crochet insider's

PASSION FOR FASHION

BY DORA OHRENSTEIN

my passion for fashion

There's no denying the beauty and creativity of crochet, from the artful laces of the Victorian era, grandma's intricate afghans of the fifties, the kooky masks and wall hangings of the seventies, to the runway fashion crochet of recent years. The question of the modern crochet designer revolves around how we can use this marvelous art to create fashions that work for us today.

Since beginning to design seriously about five years ago, I've given this question much thought, and sought answers from books and patterns anywhere they could be found. I found that there were very few "theory" books about crochet, most being collections of patterns. As wonderful as these can be, they presume a lack of curiosity on the part of the crocheter and leave a serious hole in their education. By "theory," I mean concepts and procedures that define the process of working with the materials of crochet to realize a particular design vision. When I see a good design, I want to know how it evolved from the imagination to the concrete (the designer's thought process) and which tools and techniques were employed. My aim in this book is to "unpack" my own process, which in turn may reveal elements that others can use in their creative endeavors.

We crocheters have an unbelievably rich historical tradition to draw upon—an amazing wealth of stitches and techniques at our disposal. Understanding crochet's achievements from this historical perspective can help us select those elements most suitable for today's looks and lifestyles.

—dora

contents

a bit of history

Crochet had its first heyday in the Victorian era when textile artists discovered it was a much faster way to make lace than with needles or bobbins. The craft of creating these intricate laces reached its zenith in Ireland in the late 19th and early 20th centuries, where it had been introduced as a cottage industry to allay starvation caused by the Irish famine. Crochet became fashionable everywhere when Queen Victoria accepted a gift of crocheted laces and wore them in support of the suffering Irish. In Victoria's time, crochet was widely used in collars and cuffs, baby bonnets, christening dresses, gloves, and reticules (a precursor to the handbag). These items were both lovely and practical because the very strong, delicate-looking cotton threads produced exquisitely fine work that could take both tough wear and washing.

The ease of making beautiful laces with crochet gave rise to publications of patterns for simpler versions of Irish laces. Edgings for nightgowns, undergarments, handkerchiefs, and collars and cuffs became popular with women who liked to do beautiful handiwork in their leisure time.

Aside from its uses in making lace, crochet became a popular textile craft because of its versatility in more utilitarian items. From the second half of the 19th century into the early decades of the 20th century, crochet moved from being the province of highly specialized experts into a craft shared by a larger population of hobbyists. Lifestyles and fashions changed radically after the First World War, and women wanted to make the fashions of their times; financial

constraints often demanded this. Patterns from the 1930s and '40s include bathing suits, caps, and, of course, sweaters. The yarns were not the threads of the 19th century, but far finer weight than yarns commonly used today. Unlike the lace of earlier decades, the stitches of this era were mostly closed work, plain stitches. The interest was not in the stitchery but in the styling, which was quite chic.

By the mid 20th century a new trend in crochet developed—far less fashion, and an emphasis on "home decor." Items for the home became a great vehicle for expressing crochet's possibilities: we saw lovely color work and stitchery in afghans, delicate and intricate openwork in doilies and tablecloths. But why did fashion crochet fall out of favor?

My theory is that as women entered the work force and had less leisure time, yarn companies responded by producing thicker yarns so that projects could be completed more quickly. With thicker yarns, however, it became much trickier to produce garments with good drape or flattering shape. While there have been many lovely crocheted garments in every decade right up to our own, there have also been too many boxy-looking, ill-fitting crocheted garments.

With the new renaissance of needlework, fashion crochet has made a great comeback, with many marvelous designers tackling the challenges of designing with today's fabulous new yarns.

Even more than the sister craft of knitting, crochet has an unbelievable wealth of stitch patterns— literally thousands. Tracing these variations would take years of study, but it's not hard to see why they developed. There's a marvelous flexibility and versatility in individual crochet stitches. They come in so many different sizes, from slip stitch to triples, and even greater multiples. They can be grouped together, or clustered by making a bunch of stitches in the same spot, producing such interesting shapes as fans, wheels, diamonds, petals, and more. Using chains between stitches offers the ability to make mesh patterns, on which pictures are drawn using filled in areas, as in filet crochet. The fact that one can go in any direction with crochet has led to working in the round, geometric motifs, Irish Crochet and freeform. The possibilities are infinite, and creative stitchery from the world over is collected in dazzling stitch dictionaries. Any and all of these techniques can be used to create fabulous fashion crochet.

elements of crochet design

shape

In crochetwear design, there are two elemental questions: 1) What are the qualities of the fabric? 2) What is the desired shape and also the drape of the item in question? The choices one makes in yarn, hook size, and stitch pattern will dictate the look, texture, and drape of your fabric. Shape is related to the chosen silhouette — whether full and flowing or close-fitting and tailored — what is sometimes called the cut of the clothing. How we put the pieces together is construction, which can range from a shape as simple as a rectangle to a multi-piece, highly-tailored blazer made in six or more sections.

An understanding of these elements — shape, drape, construction, and silhouette — goes a long way in achieving mastery of the fashion crochet craft. Armed with this knowledge, you can understand why patterns work or why they do not and learn to successfully indulge your own creativity. For each design presented here, I discuss these elements and how I arrived at the solutions. By making the items in this book, and/or reading the instructions I feel sure you will be more confident in deploying these elements when you make crochet fashions on your own. Over time, you will discover your own methods and strategies.

Within the infinite possibilities crochet offers, designers make choices based on their individual sense of fashion and their ideas about what constitutes good design. I'll explore both of these factors more deeply on page 7.

SHAPE AND DRAPE

Drape is one of those qualities that's hard to define, yet we know good drape when we see it. Thin, airy textiles like silk, taffeta, and muslin drape the body attractively, falling into folds around it and moving gracefully with the body's motion. The subject of drape is always a preoccupation for crochet designers, because the winding and looping of yarn inherent in crochet stitchery too easily results in fabric that is thick and stiff. With the thinner yarns of yesteryear, beautifully draped crochet clothing could be made with little difficulty, but since worsted weight yarn has become the norm in needlework, fabric that flows with the body is harder to come by.

In fact, it was because of poor drape that crochet acquired a reputation as an unsuitable vehicle for fashion. There are many reasons why boxy crochet clothing was produced in the 1970s and '80s, but perhaps the most significant was the attempt to "convert"

drape

knitting patterns to crochet. No crochet stitch should be asked to substitute for a knitted stitch — the resulting fabric will necessarily be too bulky, but pattern publishers resorted to this tactic in order to make one pattern serve both knitters and crocheters.

Because of this unfortunate era in recent crochet history, I have paid special attention to drape in all the garments in this book. Large hooks and loose stitches are used often to achieve this quality. If you find some of the hook choices surprising, I urge you to give them a try — you may be amazed at how flattering crochet clothing can be when sufficient due is paid to the quality of drape in the fabric.

GARMENT CONSTRUCTION

In each chapter of this book, we will begin with items that require little or no shaping and move gradually to more complex, structured pieces. This way, you can master a type of stitch pattern, then gradually work with it in several configurations, learning how it interacts with different yarns and uses.

Simple squares and rectangles are amazingly versatile, and nearly half the projects in this book are made with them. Wearables made from these simple shapes needn't look boxy, however. The crucial factor for wearables is the drape of the fabric: a flowing, flexible fabric will hang well on the body, showing its curves, and will move fluidly with the body rather than hang stiffly from it. The choice

of stitch pattern and hook are key elements which determine the drape of your fabric.

Garments can be put together in myriad ways, and in this book I've explored some that are more unusual. Traditionally, knit and crochetwear follow the construction of sewn garments, with a sweater consisting of separate pieces for back, front, and two sleeves. It's peculiar that this has become so pervasive, since it's not really necessary to put the pieces together this way, especially in crochet. Remember, crochet stitches can be built up in any direction, and one can easily add more fabric anywhere it's needed without a seam. In fact, in its Irish Crochet heyday, crochet clothing was made by arranging many small motifs on a pre-cut fabric pattern, then filling in the gaps between motifs with flexible "mesh" stitches, allowing the designer a great deal of freedom in how to create the end shape.

Some of the garments in this book are simple: the Ripple Resort Mini and Gotta Ruana. Some garments are constructed the traditional way with horizontal rows across the body, and many explore my favorite method, vertical construction, which I delve into at length with individual projects. You'll find a few other quirky methods, like having rows run both horizontally and vertically, as in the Caribe Coverup and Becoming Bikini, and working a large piece and then adding a sizable border all around it, as in the Big Fans Vest and Shrug. I pursue these alternatives because they add to the originality and beauty of a design. What's more, crochet is more fun and creative when you work outside the box, both literally and figuratively!

SILHOUETTES

"Two Silhouettes on the Shade" was a famous song of the doo-wop era, a time I am old enough to remember. What would those two silhouettes have looked like in the 1950s, '60s, '70s and today? Tight, close-fitting tops, and poofy skirts of the mid 20th century would have given way to a fuller silhouette, reaching its apex in the '80s with overgrown sweaters with padded shoulders, then shrinking again to the skimpier clothing of today. In fashion, the silhouette refers to the shape a garment forms around the body, and fashion eras are strongly defined by the chosen silhouette.

There is also the matter of what silhouettes are best for your body type. Not everyone on the street wearing supertight jeans is showing their figure to best advantage, are they? Most of the fashions in this book have a close-fitting silhouette, with a bit more roominess below the hips than above, probably because that's what works for my body. You can choose the silhouettes most suited to your body type by paying close attention to the actual measurements of the pieces in the schematics. Compare these to your own measurements, and you can tell how close fitting the piece is.

construction

silhouette

making a fashion statement

KNOW THYSELF

Some clothes we buy for comfort, some for practical use at work or leisure, and some simply to indulge our fashion sense. Each individual has a personal style, and the way we dress is a statement about who we are and how we wish to present ourselves to the world.

Our fashion sense usually includes a number of variables: favorite colors, shapes, and cuts that flatter our figure, age-appropriateness, and a nod, at least, to what's considered trendy. Designers, of course, have to conceive of fashions for people with preferences different from their own. We have our individual fashion sense, plus a broader view, call it an aesthetic, that governs the fashions we create. It may not even be conscious—I often learn about my work from other people's comments.

Some designers value simplicity in construction, others are drawn to the intricate. Some make very clever use of a single stitch pattern in a design, others combine stitch patterns to great effect. The qualities I personally strive for as a designer led me to the techniques used in this book.

KNOW MYSELF

I like fashions that are sophisticated yet comfortable, age neutral, sexy but tasteful, and suitable for many occasions. As a New York City native, my sensibility is definitely urban. Urban women want to look great but not pampered. We are active, we walk more than sit in a car, and we often carry packages in our arms or on our backs. Our clothes need to be stylish but easy to wear and care for, and fully functional. There's no time for sweaters that fall off the shoulders or take more than a few seconds to close. We especially like a garment that can go from work to a night out, because there's no time to change.

My clothes need to convey attractiveness, intelligence, and competence. Clothes that emphasize extreme fragility or immaturity are less appealing. Styling should take in but not necessarily give in to contemporary trends. For example, I'm likely to use the empire waist that's been fashionable for several years, because it's flattering to many figures, while I stay away from the baby doll look that I hope will go away soon.

WHAT CONSTITUTES GARMENT GREATNESS

Whether you're a city dweller or not, we're all concerned with the basic elements of what makes a garment look great when worn: good fit, flattering proportions, and attractive colors. Functionality in clothing is important, too. Your garment should be suitable to the season, both in weight and color, and adaptable to other clothing in your wardrobe. Finally, we want to make a garment that will stay in style for several seasons or more, and one that's fun to crochet. To sum this up, what I strive for in crochet fashion is based on the following criteria:

1. Looks great
2. Easy wear and easy care
3. Functional: suitable for certain weather, certain occasions and hassle-free
4. Long lasting: styles that are classic but not stodgy; fabric is durable
5. Fun to make

As for technical details of crochet design, I admire work that balances the basic elements of yarn, construction, and stitches. A garment that fits beautifully is great, one that draws the eye to the stitch pattern or color work is even better, and if it shows off a great yarn, that's a home run! Another quality I strive for is originality and innovation in style and construction.

I want my crochet designs to be something unique that you can't buy at the store. My ideal crochet wardrobe consists of items I consider very special, that are meant to stand out, even garner compliments. But a desire for praise is not the whole story: what I want my designs to communicate is my love for beautiful, handcrafted things, that are made with care. I've aimed for that in every single design in this book. I want you to love wearing my designs.

general instructions

Instructions in this book are very detailed and aim to convey information as clearly and concisely as possible. In crochet, sometimes a picture is worth a thousand words, and a good diagram may be worth even more. These are inserted whenever they can assist you.

Some conventions of instruction writing have been adapted to more closely suit the designs in this book. For example, gauge may not be given as rows and stitches equaling 4", as often a stitch pattern does not fit neatly into this interval. To promote ease of swatching and measuring, gauge is given where the pattern naturally divides at an inch or quarter-inch interval.

GAUGE AND SWATCHING

Swatching and measuring are crucial to getting good fit in your garments so I urge you not to spend all that labor and love without taking this first crucial step. Your swatch should be at least 5 to 8 repeats of a stitch pattern and as many rows. Gauge naturally changes as you work a piece and it gets heavier, so check your gauge as you work to keep it from getting too far off.

SIZING

While sizing is typically given at 4" intervals, the thicker yarns and more sophisticated stitch patterns used today require that size take into account natural dividing points in the pattern. This is the practice used here. Remember, your body isn't a size 10 or 2x—these are no more than rough measures developed by clothing manufacturers. In knitting or crochet of yesteryear, plain, small stitches were the norm, so simply adding and subtracting stitches at the ends of rows was a convenient way to tailor sizing. Because of this, the magic 4" number was easy to achieve and became the norm. As yarns and stitches have grown, sizing needs to be handled with more subtlety.

Exact measurements are given for finished pieces in several sizes. To select the size that will fit you best, please measure yourself carefully and choose the size that allows for 2"–4" of ease at the bust and/or hip. The larger your measurements, the more ease, proportionally, you will need for well-fitting garments.

SEAMS

Joining pieces is, for many, a necessary evil. Call me crazy, I actually enjoy making seams, maybe because it means I will shortly be putting on my garment for the first time. There are several commonly used seams, and each of them has its purpose.

My favorite one for most side seams, sleeve seams, or any seam which is not subjected to a great deal of pull, is mattress stitch, carefully worked from the right side, matching stitch for stitch and ensuring that stitch or color patterns line up exactly.

Lay the two pieces side by side on a flat surface with right side facing. Line up the stitches and/or rows on each piece, and pin at regular intervals. Bring your tapestry needle under one strand from one piece and then under the analogous strand on the other piece. Now, remaining on the same piece, bring the needle under the next stitch up, then under the analogous stitch on the other piece. In other words, you are going back and forth, always beginning the next stitch of the seam on the same side where you ended the previous stitch. Pull the yarn just tight enough to close any gaps, but not so tight as to cause puckering in the fabric. In most cases pick up only one strand from either side of the seam. If you pick up the strands closest together, you will see the tops of stitches, which can be a decorative element, and will add a little extra fabric if needed. You can also pick up the strands that are farther apart, or all four strands if your yarn is thin or very fuzzy. Mattress stitch is a good choice for joining sleeves to armholes, too. Picking up both strands of the stitches being connected will make the seam as invisible as possible. With bulky yarn, however, there will be a bulky seam. With thinner yarn and small stitches, working mattress stitch from the wrong side over both strands is a nice way of making a very professional-looking seam. The best way to choose the right seam is to try it on the work at hand, as different yarns and stitches will affect the result.

mattress stitch

8

Begin side seams at the bottom of the garment, leaving a long tail. At both ends of the seam, and especially at the top under an armhole, reinforce the end of the seam by weaving the tail, from the inside, horizontally back and forth across the seam for a couple of inches.

At the shoulders, which bears the weight of the garment, a single crochet or slip stitch seam is recommended when possible, worked from the wrong side. This is only impractical when a very bulky yarn is used, which would cause the seam to be thick and, well, unseemly. In that case, sew the seam first from the outside, then work it over once more from the inside for added strength. An alternative for a strong shoulder seam is a slip stitch seam. You can slip stitch through one or two strands of either side. It's best not to pull slip stitches too tightly, but match them in size to the tops of the stitches being joined.

BLOCKING AND STEAMING

Many people advocate blocking of crochet stitches, but I generally shy away from it. I like the springy look of freshly made stitches, and if you pay attention to making your stitches even, you can dispense with blocking or steaming much of the time. Of course, sometimes steaming is an absolutely necessity to get rid of curl at the edges of fabric. It's also very useful to soften fabrics that are too stiff.

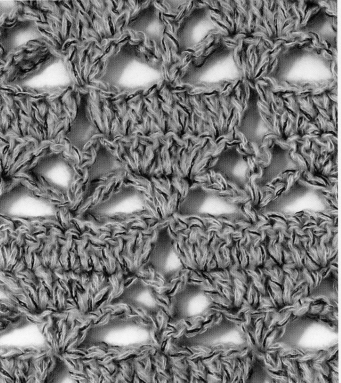

Where blocking is recommended for the designs in this book, it's for a particular reason that will be explained. If you are a fan of blocking, go ahead and do it, but be aware that it may add a little more fabric, perhaps half an inch to an inch depending on the fiber content of the yarn. Natural fibers like wool, cotton, and silk can take heat, but synthetics often can't, and many yarns of today have a mix of both. The labels on yarn will tell you whether ironing is safe for the fabric. Always start gingerly with just a little bit of steam, and do not place your iron directly on the fabric but, rather, hover over it. I purchased an iron that gives long blasts of steam just for the purpose of blocking—because it really is a must sometimes.

Enough of preliminaries! Let's turn the page and explore our mutual passion for fashion!

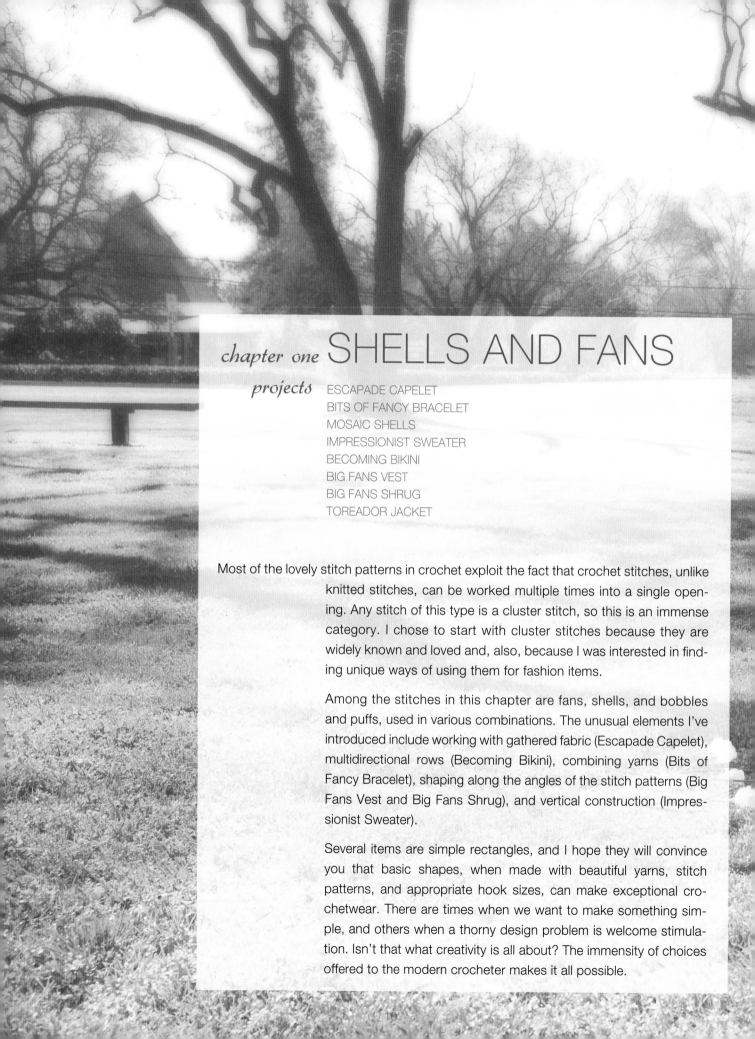

chapter one SHELLS AND FANS

projects

Most of the lovely stitch patterns in crochet exploit the fact that crochet stitches, unlike knitted stitches, can be worked multiple times into a single opening. Any stitch of this type is a cluster stitch, so this is an immense category. I chose to start with cluster stitches because they are widely known and loved and, also, because I was interested in finding unique ways of using them for fashion items.

Among the stitches in this chapter are fans, shells, and bobbles and puffs, used in various combinations. The unusual elements I've introduced include working with gathered fabric (Escapade Capelet), multidirectional rows (Becoming Bikini), combining yarns (Bits of Fancy Bracelet), shaping along the angles of the stitch patterns (Big Fans Vest and Big Fans Shrug), and vertical construction (Impressionist Sweater).

Several items are simple rectangles, and I hope they will convince you that basic shapes, when made with beautiful yarns, stitch patterns, and appropriate hook sizes, can make exceptional crochetwear. There are times when we want to make something simple, and others when a thorny design problem is welcome stimulation. Isn't that what creativity is all about? The immensity of choices offered to the modern crocheter makes it all possible.

ESCAPADE CAPELET

I've already mentioned the issue of fabric drape more than once and some of the challenges crochet presents. One good solution is to work with openwork, lacy stitches, which create a less dense fabric than do solid stitches. My desire in this capelet was to get a super-drapey fabric that could be gathered and yet feel soft and flexible. Some fabulous effects in high fashion are obtained by gathering fabric, and I've thought about how to achieve this in crochet for quite a while. For a long time, the solution eluded me. Then, in 2007, I was asked to make a trim for a gigantic sun umbrella for *knit.1* magazine. Before the monster-sized, very lacy trim was attached to its host, I discovered it lying on my worktable, gathered in many layers, looking like a gorgeous petticoat. Seeing that made me understand the answer to gathering crochet — BIG BIG HOLES. Seeking the right openwork stitch, I browsed stitch dictionaries and was drawn to the large overall patterns. These patterns are generally worked over many stitches and several rows, and though I had always found them very beautiful, I hadn't yet found the right place for them. Here was my chance to use one.

Naturally, given my obsession with Diamond shapes (see chapter 2), I fell in love with this pattern called Diamond Shells. Another piece of the design puzzle began as an urge to work with kid mohair, especially in the form of the lovely Kidlin by Louet, with its whispy romantic aura. Two pattern repeats of the Diamond Shells pattern with this yarn was very luscious, indeed, and large enough to cover half of the front of me. The mirror told me it was just the length for a capelet. As I pondered how to shape it, the answer jumped into focus—gather it. This was an exciting moment when several creative impulses merge and "go boing!"

Deciding on how the garment will close is not an easy task. If you wait until after it's done, you may lose an opportunity to make a buttonhole or other closure device. Often I'm inclined to make closures out of crochet, but this time I knew the lacy mauve capelet had to have a velvet ribbon. For one thing, pulling mohair through holes wouldn't be fun. This inspired a visit to M&J (www.mjtrim.com), the vast New York emporium of every imaginable button and trim. The perfect complementary color was found and I also picked out the rhinestone button for the little purse called Preciosilla. Don't ask what else I brought home from the shop — a designer can never have too many buttons, right? When the time comes, and I get to wear this little item, I intend to take it out for several escapades in the Big Apple!

ESCAPADE CAPELET

skill level: intermediate

finished measurements

Width, 11"
Top edge length, approximately 61"
Bottom edge length, approximately 90"

materials

Louet Kidlin, (1.75 ounces/120 yards, 50 grams/110
meters per skein): Orchard Mist — 3 skeins
Size L-11 (8.00 mm) crochet hook or size needed to
obtain gauge
2 yds — ⅝" purple velvet ribbon

gauge

1 patt rep = 8" x 8"
Note: A swatch with 2 patt reps is recommended
to familiarize yourself with this pattern.

Note: Capelet can be worn as a shawl without
the ribbon.

diamond lace pattern

This pattern was adapted with permission from a Bernat pattern.
Multiple of 16 + 5 (add 1 for foundation ch)

instructions

Row 1: Sc into 2nd ch from hook, (ch 5, sk 3 ch, sc into next ch) twice, *sk 1 ch, 5 dc into next ch, sk 1 ch, sc into next ch, ** (ch 5, sk 3 ch, sc into next ch) 3 times; rep from * ending last rep at ** when 8 ch rem, ending (ch 5, sk 3 ch, sc into next ch) twice, turn.

Row 2: *(Ch 5, sc in ch-5 loop) twice, 5 dc in next sc, sc in center dc of next fan, 5 dc in next sc, sc in next ch-5 loop, rep from * across, ending ch 5, sc in next ch-5 loop, ch 2, dc in last sc, turn.

Row 3: Ch 1, sc in dc, *ch 5, sc in ch-5 loop, 5 dc in next sc, sc in center dc of fan, ch 5, sc in center dc of next fan, 5 dc in next sc, sc in next ch-5 loop, rep from * ending ch 5, sc in last ch-5 loop, turn.

Row 4: Ch 3 (counts 1 dc), 2 dc in first sc, *sc in ch-5 loop, 5 dc in next sc, sc in center dc of next fan, ch 5, sc in next ch-5 loop, ch 5, sc in center dc of next fan, 5 dc in next sc, rep from * across, ending sc in next ch-5 loop, 3 dc in last sc, turn.

Row 5: Ch 1, sc in dc, sk 2 dc, *5 dc in next sc, sc in center dc of next fan, (ch 5, sc in ch-5 loop) twice, ch 5, sc in center dc of next fan, rep from * across ending 5 dc in next sc, sk 2 dc, sc in tch, turn.

Row 6: Ch 3 (counts as 1 dc), 2 dc in first sc, *sc in center dc of next fan, 5 dc in next sc, sc in next ch-5 loop, (ch 5, sc in next ch-5 loop) twice, 5 dc in next sc, rep from * across ending sc in center dc of next fan, 3 dc in last sc, turn.

Row 7: Ch 1, sc in dc, *ch 5, sc in center dc of next full fan, 5 dc in next sc, sc in next ch-5 loop, ch 5, sc in next ch-5 loop, 5 dc in next sc, sc in center dc of next fan, rep from * ending ch 5, sc in tch, turn.

Row 8: *Ch 5, sc in next ch-5 loop, ch 5, sc in center dc of next fan, 5 dc in next sc, sc in next ch-5 loop, 5 dc in next sc, sc in center dc of next fan, rep from * ending ch 5, sc in next ch-5 loop, ch 2, dc in last sc, turn.

Row 9: Ch 1, sc in dc, ch 5, sc in next ch-5 loop, ch 5, sc in center dc of next fan, *5 dc in next sc, sc in center dc of next fan, (ch 5, sc in next ch-5 loop) twice **, ch 5, sc in center dc of next fan, rep from * ending last rep at ** in tch loop, turn.

Capelet

Ch 133.
Rows 1–9: Work pattern stitch 8 reps across, turn.

Border

Row 10: Ch 3 (counts as dc), 2 dc in sc, sc in ch-5 loop, 5 dc in next sc, sc in next ch-5 loop, 5 dc in next sc, *sc in center dc of next fan, 5 dc in next sc, (sc in ch-5 loop, 5 dc in next sc) three times, rep from * across ending sc in center dc of next fan, (5 dc in next sc, sc in next ch-5 loop) 2 times, 3 dc in last sc, turn.

Row 11: Ch 1, sc in first dc, sk 2 dc, *5 dc in next sc, sc in center dc of next fan, rep from * across, ending sc in tch, turn.

Row 12: Ch 3, 2 dc in first sc, *sc in center dc of next fan, 5 dc in next sc, rep from * across, ending sc in center of last fan, 3 dc in last sc, end off.

Tie on at top right corner of garment into base of foundation ch, ch 3. Working into base of foundation ch, work 2 dc in sc, sc in ch-3 sp, 5 dc in next sc, sc in ch-3 sp, 5 dc in next sc, *sc in base of next fan, (5 dc in next sc, sc in next ch-3 sp) 3 times, 5 dc in next sc, rep from * ending with sc in base of next fan, (5 dc in next sc, sc in next ch-3 sp) 2 times, 3 dc in last sc, ch 1, turn work 180 degrees. Work 20 evenly-spaced sc along side edge of work, including bottom border, sl st to top of first dc on last row of border. End off. Tie on at top of opposite side edge and rep sc edging.

Ribbon Tie

Using fingers and working carefully, weave ribbon through top border row as follows: Begin at one edge, weave ribbon from front to back under 2 dc of half shell at edge (3rd dc is covered by sc edging). Bring ribbon up from back to front on other side of these 2 dc, next to the sc. You will be weaving the ribbon over all the sc in the border and under all the fans, continuing to the opposite side, where you mirror the first edge by weaving under the first 2 dc in the row.

BITS OF FANCY BRACELET

This project is a stash buster, specifically for those small remnants of fancy yarns you can't bear to throw out but don't know what to do with. Use a basic shell pattern to create a rectangle that stretches around the wrist and closes with a decorative button. When picking yarns from your stash for this project, be adventurous in blending colors and textures that aren't necessarily obvious matches. I find you can never judge this until you stitch it. This is a great project for experimenting with yarn combinations, and you might want to do several versions depending on who will be wearing it, and for what occasion. I recommend using brighter colors near the center and more neutral ones at the outer edges. You can combine yarns of varying, but not widely different thicknesses — the model has both worsted weight and chunky yarns. The project can also be done using thinner yarns for a more delicate look; simply add shells for more length as necessary to circle the wrist. The final length of the bracelet should be about 1" greater than the desired wrist circumference in order for it to overlap and close securely.

BITS OF FANCY BRACELET

skill level: beginner

finished measurements

7¼" x 3"

materials

Approximately 2–3 yds of 5 different fancy yarns,
    metallics, ribbons, all DK weight.
Model includes these Berroco yarns: Metallic FX,
    Zodiac, Cotton Twist Variegated
Size F-5 (3.75 mm) crochet hook
1 shank button, 1" in diameter
Needle and thread to match

gauge

1 patt rep = 1¼"
For this piece, yarns may have slightly different
weights and therefore gauge will vary somewhat from
row to row. Feel free to change gauge and adjust
number of shells to encircle wrist.

stitching tip

If you plan to use yarns of different weights in this
project, swatch first with the chunkiest to see what
size hook works best. When you add the thinner
yarns, match the gauge of your original swatch — this
means you have to work a bit more loosely with the
thinner yarn. If not, the rows with thinner yarns will pull
in the fabric, a result to be avoided. The ability to work
at different tensions is a fine one for the crocheter to
master, as it gives you excellent control of your work
and the finished product.

color sequence

Change color at the end of each row.
Rows 1–7: A, B, C, D, E, C, B; Color C is used for border.
Note: To change color, on the last loop before color change, draw the new color through.

shell stitch pattern

Multiple of 6 + 2

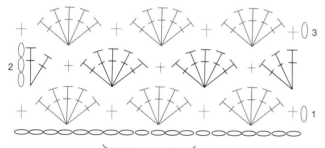

instructions

With A, ch 32.

Row 1: Sc in 2nd ch from hook, *sk 2 ch, 5-dc in next ch, sk 2 ch, sc in next ch, rep from * to end, change color, turn – 5 patt rep.

Row 2: Ch 3, 2 dc in first sc, *sk 2 dc, sc in next dc, sk 2 dc, 5 dc in sc, rep from * across, ending sk 2 dc, sc in center of next fan, sk 2 dc, 3 dc in last sc. Change color, turn.

Row 3: Ch 1, sc in first dc, sk 2 dc, *5 dc in next dc, sk 2 dc, sc in next dc, rep from * to end. Change color, turn. Ch 3.

Rows 4–7: Rep rows 2 and 3 for pattern.

finishing

Edging and Button Band

Change to edging color C on last st of 7th row, turn. Work sc edging all around, ending with 16 sc in last side edge. Turn, work sc into each of the next 6 sc, ch 4, sc into each of the next 6 st, turn. Work 6 sc, 4 sc around ch-4 sp, 6 sc to end. Finish off.

Place button for correct fit under buttonhole on opposite edge; sew on with matching thread.

MOSAIC SHELLS

Here's a chance to make a garment with no shaping, while at the same time becoming familiar with vertical construction and color work. I made this top for my mother, who is always hot and wanted something sleeveless and open at the neck. Any sport weight yarn would make a good choice.

One way to achieve drapey crochet is to pay attention to the direction of the rows. Horizontal rows are used in knitting and have become the norm for most garments, but for crochetwear I'm more drawn to vertical rows. Don't forget, crocheted rows are much more visible than knitted rows, because crocheted stitches have more dimension than knitted stitches. If you are going to have lots of lines in a garment, do you think it's more flattering for them to be horizontal or vertical? Now you're on my wavelength, right? Not only are vertical rows slimming, but the fabric will mold, cling, and move with the body more successfully, too.

Vertical construction turns shaping techniques on end — width is added to a garment by adding rows or longer stitches, and the length of the garment is controlled by the number of stitches in the row. For example, the average 8" armhole will be calculated with your stitch gauge, not your row gauge, as you would in traditional construction. In a vertically-constructed sweater, the width at the bust is determined by the total number of rows from side to side. There are several garments made vertically in this book, and I hope you'll learn to love this technique as much as I do. Once you become accustomed to this new way of thinking, the design possibilities it unlocks are quite exciting.

I have trouble making a garment using only one color, and I think it's because color really stimulates my creativity. The mosaic look in this top was achieved without using bobbins, tapestry crochet, or intarsia work. It's a familiar shell pattern, with the color changing at the end of each row, and a center panel with a different color scheme.

Two out of three colors are neutral; the third is not. Creating a design where the colors are balanced can be a challenge. In general, I advocate judicious choice of colors for a garment and avoiding many intense colors in one item.

One hardship associated with color work is the necessity to weave in many more ends. I prefer to weave them in at the end, because working ends in as I crochet slows me down too much. I turn on the television or radio and attempt to get into a meditative state of mind. I work in an orderly way all around the garment and am always pleasantly surprised when the task goes much more quickly than anticipated.

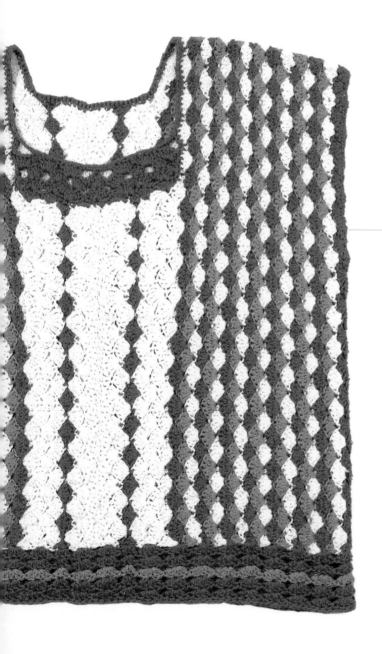

MOSAIC SHELLS

skill level: intermediate

size

Medium–Large

finished measurements

Chest, 44"

Length, 20" without border

materials

Fibranatura Oak, (1.75 ounces/175 yards, 50
  grams/160 meters per ball) 2 balls each of:
  Rust (A)
  Cream (B)
  Taupe (C)
Size E-4 (3.5 mm) crochet hook

gauge

4 patt reps = 5"

5 rows = 2"

shell stitch pattern

(see diagram page 19)
Multiple of 6 sts + 1 (add 1 for foundation ch)

Row 1: Sc in 2nd ch from hook, sk 2 ch, *5 dc in next ch, sk 2 ch, sc in next ch, rep from * across, turn.

Row 2: Ch 3, 2 dc in first sc, *sk 2 dc, sc in next dc, sk 2 dc, 5 dc in next sc; rep from * across, ending sk 2 dc, sc in next dc, sk 2 dc, 3 dc in last sc, turn.

Row 3: Ch 1, sc in first dc, sk 2 dc, *5 dc in next sc, sk 2 dc, sc in next dc, sk 2 dc; rep from * across, ending 5 dc in next sc, sk 2 dc, sc in top of tch, turn.

Rep rows 2 and 3 for patt.

color sequence guide

Color A — Rust, Color B — Cream, Color C — Taupe

Note: Work this garment in vertical rows, starting at the armhole edge. Work the back in 2 pieces to be seamed at the center. Work the front in the same way. There is no shaping except for the neckline. Use a light sport weight, summery yarn for best drape.

instructions

Back (Make 2)

With A, ch 97.

Rows 1 & 2: Work in patt for 16 patt reps, change to B.

Row 3: Work in patt across, change to C.

Row 4: Work in patt across.

Rows 5–22: Rep Rows 2–4 six times, change to A.

Row 23: Cont in patt across, change to B.

Rows 24 & 25: With B, cont in patt across.

Neckline Shaping

Rows 26–27: Cont in patt for 14 patt reps, change to A — 14 patt reps.

Row 28: Cont in patt across, change to B.

Rows 29–30: Cont in patt across.

Row 31: Cont with B, ch 1, sc in each of the first 2 dc, * hdc in next dc, dc in sc, hdc in next dc, sc in each of next 3 dc; rep from * across, ending 2 sc in last 2 dc.

Front (Make 2)

Rows 1–24: Follow directions for back.

Neckline Shaping

Rows 25–27: With color B, cont in patt for 11 patt reps, change to A.

Row 28: Cont in patt across, change to B.

Rows 29–30: Cont in Shell patt across.

Row 31: Cont with B, ch 1, sc in each of the first 2 dc, * hdc in next dc, dc, in sc, hdc in next dc, sc in each of next 3 dc; rep from * across, ending 2 sc in last 2 dc.

finishing

Sew halves of front and back together from RS with mattress stitch. Sew side seams in same manner.

Front Neckline Trim

With RS facing, tie on with A at right corner of neckline. Work sc trim along RS of neckline, over shoulder, around back of neck and down left shoulder, ch 1. Now beg working across front of neckline opening. After each row, you will slip stitch into this sc edging to move up to the next row.

Row 1: (5 dc in side of next sc row) 2 times, sk striped row, work 8 sc evenly spaced to center, 1 sc in center, 8 sc before next stripe; sk striped row, (5 dc in side of next sc row) 2 times, sl st over 2 sc on edging at left, ch 1, turn.

Row 2: (5 dc in center of fan) 2 times, 5 dc in sc, sk 3 sc, in next sc, sk 3 sc, 5 dc in center sc, sk 3 sc, sc in next sc, sk 3 sc, 5 dc in last sc, (5 dc in center of next fan) 2 time, sl st over 2 sc in right edging, ch 1 turn.

Row 3: 5 dc in center of each fan across, ch 1, sl st over 2 sc of left edging, ch 1, turn.

Row 4: 5 dc in ch-1 sp, (5 dc between next 2 fans) two times, ch 2, sc in center dc of next fan, ch 2 (dc between next 2 fans) 2 times, 5 dc in final ch-1 sp, sl st over 3 st at right edging.

Row 5: Ch 5, sk 4 dc, sc in next dc, in next fan (sc in first dc, sk 1 dc, sc in next dc, sk 1 dc, sc in last dc) 2 times, sc in ch-2 sp, sc in sc, sc in ch-2 sp, in next fan (sc in first dc, sk 1 dc, sc in next dc, sk 1 dc, sc in last dc) 2 times, sc in first dc of last fan, ch 5, sl st to sc at left edging, end off.

Bottom Border

Row 1: With RS facing, tie A on at bottom edge of Row 2, ch 3, 4 dc in same place, *sk 1 row, 5 dc in edge of next row, rep from * to center, sk 2 rows at center, then continue working 5 dc fans into every other row around, sl st to top of starting ch 3.

Row 2: Ch 3, 4 dc in center dc of first fan, 5 dc in center dc of each fan around, sl st to top of starting ch 3, change to color C.

Row 3: Rep row 2, change to A.

Rows 4 & 5: Rep row 2.

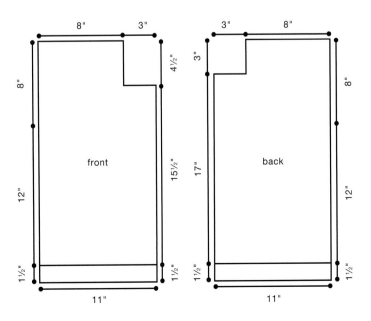

IMPRESSIONIST SWEATER

I fell in love with the painterly dabbled colors in the Zitron Ecco Aquarelle yarn and learned that the gentleman whose name is on the label — Herr Zitron, of Germany — is known for his artful dyeing techniques. The delicate colors suggested spring flowers, leading me to one of my favorite stitch patterns, which I call "leaf stitch." Swatched in this stitch, the colors morphed into separate little leaves, reminding me of Impressionist painting. I envisioned a blousy, feminine sweater, with a deep V-neck, full sleeves falling to just below the elbow, and a loose, flowing silhouette.

The leaf stitch pattern is a type of cluster stitch. Clusters, by definition, crowd several stitches into a small space, creating shapes resembling shells, fans, and other pleasingly curvy images. Condensing stitches in this way tends to thicken the fabric. To counter this, I used a much larger hook than one would normally choose for DK weight yarn. With this strategy, you get large stitches and a very drapey, stretchy fabric; each size will fit a range of bodies. With these loosely woven stitches, it's important not to stretch the garment unduly and store it folded rather than on a hanger.

It might not be obvious at first glance, but this garment is constructed vertically, meaning the rows go from top to bottom rather than across. I explain some of the principles in connection with the Mosaic Shells top (project on page 22). In this more tailored piece, several different techniques are used to shape the waist, sleeves, and neckline.

To narrow the fabric at the waist in traditional horizontal construction, one would decrease stitches at the garment's sides. In the vertical construction used here, one way to narrow at the waist is to change the height of stitches. Since the stitch pattern incudes double crochets, I dropped the pattern and used only single crochet stitches for several inches in the waist area, but only in a few rows, resulting in gentle waist shaping.

For the sleeves, I needed a method for bringing in the fullness at the cuff and came up with two: first is the same strategy used for waist shaping, bringing the stitch pattern down to plain single crochets, done on all rows, to create the cuff. To add even more sleeve fullness, short rows were inserted at regular intervals. Short rows are simply rows that are not as long as those around them — work to a designated point then turn back before reaching the end of the row. Here the short rows go right up to the cuff before turning back, creating a gathered look one sees more commonly in sewn garments than crochetwear.

The leaf stitch pattern and several other stitch patterns explored in this book has a built-in angle. I love angles because they can be exploited in shaping. In this design, the slanted part of the armhole, the neckline, and the sleeve cap all use this strategy.

A fitted armhole is created by making increases at the top of rows for the first several rows of the pattern. After completing the necessary rows for the slanted part of the armhole, we add some chains for the straight part of the armhole and work into them in the next row. In the rows following, we create a slope for the shoulder by adding one stitch at the top in the next few rows. Once there is a sufficient number of rows for the shoulders, we begin the decrease to create the V-neck.

To make the sleeves that will fit into this armhole, there is an increase in the first few rows made in the exact same way as for the armhole. This upper section of the sleeve is called the sleeve cap. The top of it is flat and will fit into the straight part of the armhole. At the end of the sleeve, we will decrease the same number of patterns, so the sleeve can fit into the back of the armhole.

One technical point about angled shaping: although the increase and decrease patterns remove stitches at the same rate — one pattern every two rows — the appearance of the slant is not exactly the same. Try a swatch following the increase and decrease instructions, and you'll see what I mean. An exact match of the angle is crucial for the V-neck at the front. For this reason the front and back pieces are made in two halves, so that the two sides of the neckline are exact mirror images. Note that a V-neck top should have a high neck at the back. Without it, the top will tend to slide off the shoulders.

I'd like to think this design is timeless, a feminine, flattering, versatile piece that can find a place in your wardrobe for a long time to come.

IMPRESSIONIST SWEATER

skill level: intermediate

size
Small–Medium (Large–1x, 2x–3x)

finished measurements
Chest, 36 (44, 52)"
Armhole depth, 6 (7, 8)"
Sleeves, 13 (14½, 16)" armhole to cuff

materials
Zitron Ecco Yarn, (1.75 ounces/120 yards, 50 grams/110 meters per ball): Green/Pink/Yellow Multi-color — 12 (14, 16) balls
Size K-10.5 (6.5 mm) crochet hook

gauge
2 patt and 2 rows = 2"

leaf stitch

Multiple of 3 + 1 (add 1 for foundation ch)

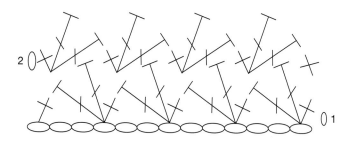

Row 1: Ch 1, *(sc, 2 dc) in first st, sk 2 sts, rep from * ending with sc in last st, turn.

Row 2: Ch 1, *(sc, 2 dc) in first sc, sk 2 sts, rep from * ending with sc in last sc, turn.

Rep row 2 for pattern.

shaping technique

Note: Stitch counts are given in number of patt reps. Always end row with sc in last sc unless otherwise instructed.

Increase (1 patt rep)
End row with (sc, 2 dc) in last sc, ch 2, turn.
Next row: (Sc, 2 dc) in 2nd ch from hook, cont in patt.

Decrease (1 patt rep)
Ch 1, sk sc, sl st in ea of next 2 dc, beg patt in next sc.
Next row work even in patt.

instructions

Waist Shaping
Work designated number of patt reps, sc in next sc, sc in each of next 8 sts; in next sc cont in patt.

In next row work in patt to waist shaping, [sk 2 sc, (sc, 2 dc) in next sc] 3 times; cont in patt.

Short Rows for Sleeve
First short row: Work in patt to within last 7 sc, leave them unworked, ch 1. Turn.

Second short row: Sk sc, sl st in ea of next 2 dc, beg patt in next sc. Next row will be a full row; work in patt, placing last sc in same st as first short row, sc into ea sc of row before short rows.

Half Back (Make 2)
Ch 38 (41, 44).
Rows 1 & 2: Work in patt across — 12 (13, 14) patt reps.

Begin Armhole Shaping
Row 3: Work in patt, ending row with ch 2, turn.
Row 4: (Sc, 2 dc) in 2nd ch from hook, cont with 7 (8, 9) patt reps, work waist shaping patt, cont in patt ending with sc in last sc.
Rows 5–6 (8, 10): Rep rows 3 & 4 — 14 (16, 18) patt reps.

Shape Straight Part of Armhole
Row 7 (9, 11): Work in patt to end, ch 13.
Row 8 (10, 12): Beg in 2nd ch from hook, work in patt over added st, completing a total of 12 (14, 16) patt reps, work waist shaping patt, cont in patt ending with sc in last sc.

Shoulder Shaping
Row 9 (11, 13): Work in patt across, 2 sc in last sc, turn — 18 (20, 22) patt reps.
Row 10 (12, 14): Ch 1, sc in first sc, beg patt in next sc, cont in patt to end.
Row 11 (13, 15): Work in patt across, sc in last 2 sc, turn.
Row 12 (14, 16): Ch 1, sc in sc, beg patt in next sc, cont in patt completing 12 (14, 16) patt; work waist shaping patt; cont in patt to end.

Size Large–1X
Rows 15 & 16: Work even in patt.

Size 2X–3X
Rows 17 & 18: Work even in patt.

Shape Back Neckline
Row 13 (17, 19): Work even in patt.
Row 14 (18, 20): Ch 1, sk sc, sl st in ea of next 2 dc, beg patt in next sc, cont in patt to end — 17 (19, 21) patt reps.
Rows 15 (19, 21)–18 (22, 24): Work in patt completing 17 (20, 23) patt reps.

Half Front (Make 2)
Rep instructions for back from rows 1–12 (14, 16).

Shape Neckline
Row 13 (17, 19): Work in patt completing 15 (18, 21) patt reps, sc in next sc, turn.
Row 14 (18, 20): Ch 1, sk sc, sl st in ea of next 2 dc, beg patt in next sc, cont in patt to end.
Row 15 (19, 21): Work in patt completing 14 (17, 20) patt reps, sc in next sc, turn.
Row 16 (20, 22): Ch 1, sk sc, sl st in ea of next 2 dc, beg patt in next sc, work 7 (10, 13) patt reps, sc in next sc, work shaping patt with sc in ea of next 8 st, in next sc cont in patt to end.
Row 17 (21, 23): Work in patt completing patt reps, sc in next sc, turn — 12 (14, 16) patt reps.
Row 18 (22, 24): Rep row 14.

Sleeve (Make 2)
Note: Stitch counts below are for changing number of patt reps. Number of sc at bottom (cuff) of sleeve remains constant throughout.
Ch 42 (47, 52).
Row 1: Sc in 2nd ch from hook and in ea of next 6 (8, 10) ch, beg patt in next ch, work in patt to end, beg inc patt — 11 (12, 13) patt reps.

Row 2: Complete inc, cont in patt to last 7 (9, 11) sc, sc in ea sc, turn — 12 (13, 14) patt reps.

Rows 3: Ch 1, sc next 7 (9, 10) sc, beg patt in next sc, work in patt to end, beg inc patt.

Row 4: Complete inc, cont in patt to last 7 (9, 10) sc, sc in ea sc, ch 1, turn — 13 (14, 15) patt reps.

Row 5: Cont in established patt, with inc patt.

Rows 6–7 (9, 11): Work short rows, cont inc patt — 14 (15, 16) patt reps.

Rows 8 (10, 12)–31 (33, 35): (Work even for 6 rows, then work 2 short rows) 3 times.

Rows 32 (34, 36)–33 (35–37): Beg dec patt — 13 (15, 16) patt reps.

Rows 34 (36, 38)–37 (39, 41): Cont dec patt — 13 (14, 15) patt reps–12 (13, 14) patt reps.

Row 38 (40, 42)–39 (41, 43): Work short rows, cont dec patt — 11 (12, 13) patt reps.

Note: There will be one less patt rep at end because 2nd short row is always 1 rep less.

finishing

Sew halves of front and back together on RS using mattress stitch, picking up one topmost strand from each half. For strength and stability at shoulders, join shoulders from WS with slip stitch seam. Sew side seams. Pin sleeves to armholes, matching slanted part of sleeve cap to slanted part of armhole and distributing any excess in sleeve evenly, then sew from inside with mattress stitch. Sew seams of sleeves.

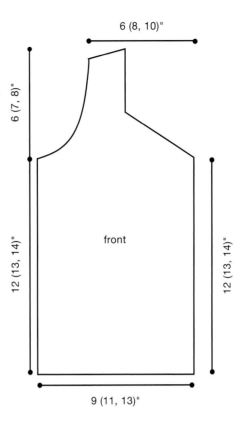

front

6 (8, 10)"

6 (7, 8)"

12 (13, 14)"

12 (13, 14)"

9 (11, 13)"

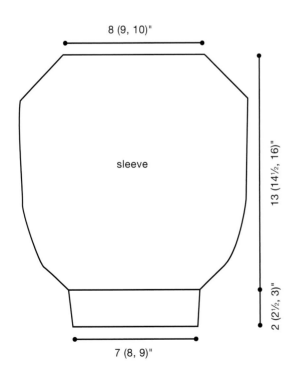

sleeve

8 (9, 10)"

13 (14½, 16)"

2 (2½, 3)"

7 (8, 9)"

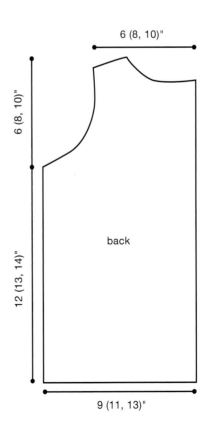

back

6 (8, 10)"

6 (8, 10)"

12 (13, 14)"

9 (11, 13)"

BECOMING BIKINI

The nature of a bikini — a body-hugging item that needs to cover very specific body parts — brings us further into the challenges of garment construction. Construction is all about the shape you need to make and the techniques you will use to achieve that shape. I've wanted to tackle a bikini for a long time and have closely scrutinized the construction of any crocheted bikini I see. There are many methods for making bra cups, but not all of them are equally flattering. I believe the cup should resemble the shape of what's under it, and I chose the construction I think does this best: begin at the center of the cup with a line about as long as the distance from the bottom of the breast to the point, then work outward in semi-circles. This is like working in the round except it's half an oval instead of a full circle.

In circular construction, used commonly for crocheted hats, you begin with a small circle and add stitches in each subsequent round to keep the fabric growing out from that center point. For a bra cup, a perfectly round circle is not the ideal shape. Rather, you want more of a triangle at the top and a straight edge at the bottom. We have our starting line which runs from the nipple down, and we want to increase at the top but stay flat at the bottom. We do this by increasing stitches at a center point at the top to shape the cup and stay flat at the bottom. In hatmaking, where we want a flat top, we generally add the same number of stitches in each round, so that the circumference is growing in correct proportion to the radius (that's about all I remember of high school math!) To make it pointy, we will be stingier with our stitches. At the start of the bra, you add fewer stitches at each increase; then, in later rows, you add more stitches to form a gentler cup shape.

Of course cup shape is only one of many concerns in bikini construction. There's the question of connecting the cups, the closure at the back, and straps. Closure for both top and bottom is much trickier than with store-bought suits, where the super stretchy fabric clings by itself. A crocheted bikini needs secure fastening, without adding too much hardware. For the bikini bottom, you need to cover more square footage in the back than in the front, so unlike sweaters, the front and back will be shaped quite differently.

My design decisions were dictated by several additional considerations. Only the very young and skinny can get away with lots of bottom showing, so I aimed for a style that's sexy and flattering for various figures — the shorts look that's become popular. As for closures and stability of the garment, I wanted a real band around the bra to keep the cups from sliding around and closures that would be adjustable to many bodies without looking flimsy.

With all this in mind I found a lovely thin cotton, Vintage Cotton by Karabella, that makes the suit practical and allowed for some pretty stitch work. It makes more sense to use fine yarn in a small garment like this, and small stitches are good for keeping the garment's shape over time, especially one that will be subjected to water often. I looked for a stitch pattern with really closed fabric. The clusters in this pattern create nice texture and also serve to highlight details of the construction. Look closely, and you can see that the rows run in a half circle on the bra, vertically on the bottom and with a horizontal band on both. For more perfect coverage and precise shaping at the crotch, a separate flap of single crochet was made. Using vertical rows on the bikini bottom made it easy to control the relative size of the front and back, with rows longer at the back where there is more to cover. To decrease the amount of fabric closer to the waist, I used a smaller version of the cluster stitch at the top of every other row: double crochet clusters became half double puffs.

To make the bikini adaptable to many bodies, I used string ties at the hip and shoulder straps. Rather than a string of single crochet stitches, I had fun inventing a way to make a string based on the leaf stitch pattern.

BECOMING BIKINI

skill level: intermediate

size

Small (Medium, Large)

finished measurements

Bust, 32–34 (36–38, 40–42)"
Hips, 34–35 (36–38, 40–42)"

materials

Karabella Vintage Cotton Yarn (1.75 ounces/140
   yards, 50 grams/130 meters per ball):
   #340 Straw — 5 (6, 8) balls
Size B-1 (2.25 mm) crochet hook or size needed to obtain
   gauge

gauge

Note: Gauge is different for top and bottom because of
additional sc rows in stitch pattern for bottom.
Bra
5 (CL, ch 1) in pattern = 2" and 8 rows in pattern = 3"
Bottom
3 (CL, ch 1) in pattern, 1 row CL and 3 rows sc = 1"

special stitches

Cluster (CL): (Yo, insert hook in designated st, pull up loop, yo, draw through 2 lps on hook) 3 times, yo, draw through all 4 lps on hook to complete the stitch.

2-dc Cluster (2-dc CL): (Yo, insert hook in designated st, pull up loop, yo, draw through 2 lps on hook) 2 times, yo, draw through all 3 lps on hook to complete the stitch.

Puff Stitch: Yo, insert hook in designated st, pull up lp, (yo, pull up lp) 2 times (7 lps on hook), yo, pull through all lps on hook.

2 Cluster stitches together (CL2tog): (Yo, insert hook in designated st, pull up loop, yo, draw through 2 lps on hook) 3 times, sk sc, (Yo, insert hook in next st, pull up loop, yo, draw through 2 lps on hook) 3 times, yo, pull through all 7 lps on hook.

Single crochet 2 stitches together (sc2tog): Insert hook into designated stitch, yo, pull up loop, insert hook into next stitch, yo, pull up loop, yo, draw loop through all 3 lps on hook.

Treble crochet (tr): (Yo) 2 times, insert hook into designated stitch, yo, pull yarn through stitch (4 lps on hook), (yo, draw through 2 lps) 3 times.

instructions

Patt Stitch for Bikini Bottom

Row 1: Ch 3, 2-dc CL in first st *ch 1, sk next sc, CL in next st, rep from * to end.

Rows 2–4: Ch 1, sc across, turn.

Row 5: (Ch 1, puff in sc, ch 1, sk sc) 2 times, ch 1, *(CL, ch 1, sk next sc) rep from * across, ending with CL, turn.

Rows 6–8: Ch 1, sc across, turn.

Increase Pattern for Bottom Back

Row 1: Ch 3, 2-dc CL in first st *ch 1, sk next sc, CL in next st, rep from * across to last sc, (CL, ch 1, CL) in last sc, turn.

Row 2: Ch 1, sc across, turn.

Row 3: Ch 1, sc in ea st across, 2 sc in last sc, turn.

Row 4: Ch 1, 2 sc in first st, sc in ea sc across, turn.

Row 5: Ch 1, puff st in sc, ch 1, sk next sc; puff st in next sc, sk sc, ch 1, *(CL, ch 1, sk next sc) rep from * across to last sc, (CL, ch 1, CL) in last sc, turn.

Rows 6–8: Rep rows 2–4.

Bra Cup (Make 2)

Ch 15 (19, 23).

Row 1: Sc in 2nd ch and next 13 ch, 3 sc in next ch, turn work 180 degrees and work 1 sc in base of each st — 29 (37, 45) sc.

Row 2: Ch 3 (counts as 1 dc) 2 dc cluster in first sc, (ch 1, sk next sc, CL in next sc) 6 (8, 10) times, ch 1, sk next sc, work (CL, ch 1, CL, ch 1, CL) in next sc (center), (ch 1, sk next sc, CL in next sc) 7 (9, 11) times, turn — 17(21, 25) CL.

Row 3: Ch 1, sc in each st around, turn — 33 (41, 49) sc.

Row 4: Ch 3 (counts as 1 dc) 2 dc cluster in first sc, (ch 1, sk next sc, CL in next sc) 7 (10,12) times, ch 1, sk next sc, work (CL, ch 1, CL, ch 1, CL) in next sc (center), (ch 1, sk next sc, CL in next sc) 8 (10, 12) times, turn — 19 (23, 27) CL.

Row 5: Rep row 3—37 (45, 53) sc.

Row 6: Ch 3 (counts as 1 dc) 2 dc cluster in first sc, (ch 1, sk next sc, CL in next sc) 8 (10, 12) times, ch 1, sk next sc, work (CL, ch 1) 4 times in next sc (center), sk next sc, CL in next sc, (ch 1, sk next sc, CL in next sc) 8 (10, 12) times, turn — 22 (26, 30) CL.

Row 7: Rep row 3—43 (51, 59) sc.

Row 8: Ch 3 (counts as 1 dc) 2 dc cluster in first sc, (ch 1, sk next sc, CL in next sc) 9 (12, 14) times, ch 1, sk next sc, work [(CL, ch 1, CL, ch 1) in next sc, sk next sc] 2 times, CL in sc, (ch 1, sk next sc, CL in next sc) 10 (12,14) times, turn — 24 (28, 32) CL.

Row 9: Rep rows 3—47 (55, 63) sc.

Row 10: Ch 3 (counts as 1 dc) 2 dc cluster in first sc, (ch 1, sk next sc, CL in next sc) 11 (13, 15) times, ch 1, work (CL, ch 1, CL, ch 1, CL) in next sc, ch 1, CL in next sc, (ch 1, sk next sc, CL in next sc) 11 (13, 15) times, turn — 27 (31, 35) CL.

Row 11: Rep rows 3—53 (61, 69) sc.

Small Only

Row 12: Ch 3 (counts as 1 dc) 2-dc cluster in first sc, (ch 1, sk next sc, CL in next sc) 12 times, ch 1, sk next sc, work (CL, ch 1) 4 times in next sc (center), sk next sc, CL in next sc, (ch 1, sk next sc, CL in next sc) 12 times, turn — 30 CL.

Row 13: Rep row 3, ch 44 — 60 sc.

Small Only

Ch 24 for bust band, end off.

Medium and Large Only

Rows 12–13 (12–15): Rep rows 10–11.

Row 14 (16): Rep row 12, ch 28 (32), end off — 65 (73) sc.

Row 15 (17): Rep row 13.

Second Cup

Work second cup, do not end off, cont with bust band.

Bust Band

Ch 24 (28, 32), turn.

Row 1: Ch 1, sc in 2nd ch from hook and in each ch across; with RS facing, cont working sc into bottom edge of cup, working 1 sc in each sc row, 2 sc in each CL across each cup. Work in same manner along 2nd cup, being certain that RS is facing; then cont working sc into each ch to opposite end of band, turn — 122 (144, 164) sc.

Row 2: Ch 3 (counts as 1 dc), 2-dc Cl in first sc, *ch 1, sk next sc, CL in next sc; rep from * across, turn — 62 (72, 82) CL.

Row 3: Ch 1, sc across, at end of row, sc into side of band, sl st to find ch, end off — 122 (130, 138) sc.

String Tie for Bust Band

Tie on end at center of band, *ch 1, sc in same st, ch 4, tr2tog in sc, rep from * to desired length of tie (13–18 reps.) Rep on opposite side. Use loose ends to reinforce attachment between tie and band.

Shoulder Straps

The shoulder strap will begin at top point of bra and attach to the band at the back at the intersection where the wide part of bra band ends and the skinny part begins.

Try on bra and measure this distance. Tie on at top point of bra and work same strap as above for tie of band to measurement just made, ending with sc, ch 6, sl st to sc, ch 1, 7 sc in 6-ch ring, sl st into side of sc, end off. Slip ring just made over skinny part of band. Rep on opposite side.

Bikini Bottom Front

Note: For less fabric at upper hip, every other CL row will start with smaller st, as in row 6, both in front and back.

Front

Ch 20 (24, 28).

Row 1: Sc in second ch from hook and each ch across, turn—19 (23, 27) sts.

Row 2: Ch 3 (counts as 1 dc), 2-dc CL in 1 st sc, * sk next sc, ch 1, CL in next sc; rep from * across, turn — 10 (12, 14) CL.

Row 3–5: Ch 1, sc in each st across, turn — 19 (23, 27) sts.

Rows 7–9: Rep rows 3–5 — 23 (27, 31) sts.

Rows 10–65 (73, 81): Rep rows 2–9 — 7 (8, 9) times.

Rows 66–67 (74–75, 82–83): Rep rows 3 & 4.

Bottom Back

Ch 20 (24, 28).

Shape Right Leg

Row 1: Sc in 2nd ch from hook and in each ch across, turn — 19 (23, 27) sts.

Row 2: Work row 1 of inc patt ending with 11, (13, 15) CL, turn.

Rows 3–5: Cont with rows 2–4 of inc patt ending with 23 (27, 31) sc, turn.

Row 6: Cont with row 5 of inc patt ending with 13 (15, 17) CL (counting puffs as CL), turn.

Rows 7–9: Cont with rows 6–8 of inc patt ending with 27 (31, 35) sc, turn.

Rows 10–17: Rep rows 2–9, ending with 35 (39, 43) sc, turn.

Row 18: Work row 1 of inc patt, turn — 19 (21, 23) CL.

Medium and Large Only

Rows 19–22: Cont with rows 2–5 of inc patt. You will have 43 (47) sc at the end of row 21 and 21 (23) CL at the end of row 22, turn.

Large Only

Row 23–26: Cont with rows 7–9 of inc patt.

Row 26: Rep row 2 — 25 CL.

Shape Crotch

Small and Large Only

Rows 19–21 (27–29): Ch 1, sc in each st across, turn — 37 (41, 45) sts.

Row 22 (26, 30): Ch 1, puff st in sc, ch 1, sk next sc sc; puff st in next sc, sk next sc, ch 1, (2-dc CL, ch 1, sk next sc) 2 times, *(CL, ch 1, sk next sc) rep from * across, ending with CL in last sc, turn.

Rows 23 (31)–25 (33): Rep rows 19–21.

Row 26 (34): Ch 3, (counts as 1 dc) 2-dc CL in 1st sc, *sk next sc, ch 1, CL in next sc; rep from * across, turn.

Rows 27–42 (35—50): Rep rows 19–26 two times.

Rows 43–49 (51–57): Rep rows 19–25.

Medium Only

Rows 23–25: Ch 1, sc in each st across, turn — 45 sts.

Row 26: Ch 3, (counts as 1 dc) 2-dc CL in 1st sc, *sk next sc, ch 1, CL in next sc; rep from * across, turn — 23 CL.

Rows 27–29: Rep rows 23 — 25.

Row 30: Ch 1, puff st in sc, ch 1, sk next sc; puff st in next sc, sk next sc, ch 1, *CL, ch 1, sk next sc, rep from * across, ending with CL in last sc, turn.

Rows 31–46: Rep rows 23–30 twice.

Rows 47–53: Rep rows 23–29.

Shape Left Leg

Small Only

Row 50: Ch 3, (counts as 1 dc) 2-dc CL in 1st sc, *sk next sc, ch 1, CL in next sc; rep from * across to last 3 sts, CL2tog, turn — 18 CL.

Row 51: Ch 1, sc in each st across, turn.

Row 52: Ch 1, sc across to last 2 sts, sc2tog, turn — 34 sts.

Row 53: Ch 1, sc in each st across. turn.

Rows 54: Ch 1, puff st in sc, ch 1, sk next sc sc; puff st in next sc, sk next sc, ch 1, (2-dc CL, ch 1, sk next sc) 2 times, *(CL, ch 1, sk next sc) rep from * across to last 3 sts, CL2tog, turn.

Rows 55–57: Rep rows 51–53 — 30 sts at the end of row 57.

Rows 58–65: Rep rows 50–57.

Row 66: Rep row 50.

Row 67: Rep row 51 — 19 sts.

Shape Right Leg

Medium Only

Row 54: Ch 1, puff st in sc, ch 1, sk next sc; puff st in next sc, sk next sc, ch 1, *CL, ch 1, sk next sc, rep from * across to last 3 sts, CL2tog, turn — 18 CL (counting puffs as CL).

Row 55: Ch 1, sc in each st across, turn.

Row 56: Ch 1, sc across to last 2 sts, sc2tog, turn — 33 sts.

Row 57: Ch 1, sc in each st. across, turn.

Row 58: Ch 3, (counts as 1 dc) 2-dc CL in 1st sc, *sk next sc, ch 1, CL in next sc; rep from * across to last 3 sts, CL2tog, turn — 16 CL.

Rows 59–60: Rep rows 55 and 56 — 29 sts.

Rows 61: Rep row 57.

Rows 62–75: Rep rows 54–61 ending on row 59 — 23 sts.

Shape Left Leg
Large

Row 58: Ch 3, (counts as 1 dc) 2-dc CL in 1st sc, *sk next sc, ch 1, CL in next sc; rep from * across to last 3 sts, CL2tog, turn — 24 CL.

Row 59: Ch 1, sc in each st across, turn.

Row 60: Ch 1, sc across to last 2 sts, sc2tog, turn — 42 sts.

Row 61: Ch 1, sc in each st across, turn.

Row 62: Ch 1, puff st in sc, ch 1, sk next sc; puff st in next sc, ch 1, sk next sc, *CL, ch 1, sk next sc, rep from * across to last 3 sts, CL2tog, turn — 22 CL (counting puffs as CL).

Row 63: Rep row 59.

Rows 64–65: Rep rows 60–62.

Rows 66–83: Rep rows 58–65 ending on row 59 — 27 sc.

Mark RS of front and back pieces (sides that have more pronounced clusters).

Crotch Piece

With RS facing, work sc edging along bottom of front and back, working 2 sc in each CL row and 1 sc in each sc row.

Count 11 (13, 15) st on either side of center point of front.

Row 1: Tie on with WS facing and sc over each st just counted, turn — 22 (26, 30) sc.

Row 2: Ch 1, sc in each st across, turn.

Row 3: Ch 1, sc2tog, sc across to last 2 sts, sc2tog, turn — 20 (24, 28) sc.

Rows 4–11 (13, 15): Rep rows 2 and 3 four (5, 6) times, ending with 12 (14, 16) sc.

Rows 12–30 (14–32, 16–34): Work even on 12 (14, 16) st for 19 (19, 19) rows.

Row 31 (33, 35): Ch 1, 2 sc in first st, sc across, end with 2 sc in last sc — 14 (16, 18) sts.

Row 32 (34, 36): Ch 1, sc in each st across, turn.

Rows 33–28 (35–42, 37–46): Rep rows 31 and 32 three (4, 5) times, ending with 20 (24, 28) st. End off.

finishing

Carefully center crotch piece along bottom back piece and pin in place. Working from WS, work sl st seam to join crotch to bottom back.

From WS, make sl st side seams to join bottom front and back, picking up 1 strand from each side and matching sts to size of sc (avoid working too tightly).

With RS facing, tie on at bottom of one side seam, ch 1, work row of sc all around leg opening. End off and rep on other leg.

Hip Band

Rnd 1: Tie on at seam with RS facing, ch 1, sc in same st, work 1 sc in side of each sc row, 2 sc in side of each dc CL row, 1 sc in side of each puff, for a total of 76 (88, 100) sts on each side, 152 (176, 200) around; sl st to first sc, turn.

Rnd 2 (WS): Ch 3, *CL, ch 1, sk sc; rep from * around, turn — 76 (88, 100) CL.

Rnd 3 (RS): Sc in each st around.

Rnd 4 (RS): Sc in each st around.

Cord for Bottom

*Ch 5, tr in 4th ch from hook, rep from * until cord measures approximately 50–60". Weave cord through stitches in row 2 of hip.

about edging

Many crochet pieces are finished with single crochet edging, often worked into the sides of rows, with instructions specifying "evenly spaced stitches." When working into the sides of rows, place one single crochet in a single crochet row, two in a half double row, three in a double crochet row, etc. These are not hard and fast rules, however. With edging you can control a lot about the fit of a garment. A neckline that's too large is pulled in by working a tighter edging of single crochet or slip stitches with a smaller hook. This also works for armholes or any opening that needs a closer fit. Likewise, a sweater that is snug at the hips will ease up if a looser edging is worked around the bottom. The number of stitches in the edging is dictated by the need to tighten or loosen the fabric or match it to a stitch pattern.

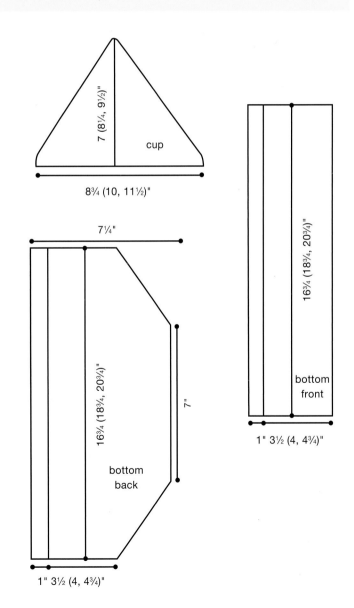

7 (8¼, 9½)"
cup
8¾ (10, 11½)"

7¼"

16¾ (18¾, 20¾)"
bottom front
1" 3½ (4, 4¾)"

16¾ (18¾, 20¾)"
7"
bottom back
1" 3½ (4, 4¾)"

BIG FANS

One of my goals in this book is to give the reader opportunities to work with many different kinds of yarns like Teva Durham's Loop-d-Loop "Shale." The interesting structure and texture of this yarn, along with its bulk, represented a challenge to me, one that led me straight to the stitch dictionary. I wanted a large "overall" pattern that could stand up to the yarn, yet live harmoniously with it, and an openwork stitch, to ensure the fabric would have drape despite the yarn's heft. When I swatched up this big fan pattern, it fit the bill exactly. The "pictures" in the pattern really popped, the yarn itself looked shimmering and plush, and the angles in the pattern provided fertile ground for designing. In the introduction to this book I discussed balancing the elements of yarn, stitch pattern, shape, and drape, and I felt I had found a good solution with these big fans.

Some designers with an architectural mindset have an enviable ability to visualize a whole garment in their imaginations, but I am not one of them. I like to make a large swatch and then stand at the mirror moving it this way and that on my body, a process that helps me make crucial design decisions about the direction of rows, placement of neckline, sleeve length, and the like.

I also like to use shapes in the stitch pattern to form the edges of pieces and put these shapes in my sample swatch so I can play with them. There is a distinct angle in this stitch pattern that I wanted to exploit for shaping the garment. In a large pattern such as these big fans, creating this slant requires decreasing over three rows.

The resulting shape in my swatch was a long diagonal that could easily become a raglan yoke. The slant was, however, too steep for shaping the torso. This guided my decison to make a main piece with the big fans pattern, using the diagonal to shape the armhole; for shaping the torso, I made a border of several rounds of double crochet all around this main piece. This offset the big fans very nicely. Finally, I added a triangular gusset for extra fabric at the hips.

Since openwork of this type creates a garment that provides more adornment than warmth, I thought a vest was the right choice, and because of the wide border, a long line vest made good fashion sense. A short band of stitches connects the front and back pieces over the shoulder.

Because I depend on the natural slant of the pattern to create the armhole, this pattern is not as adaptable for sizing as some others. Women with more ample measurements around the chest do not have correspondingly large shoulders, so designs generally create a steeper angle at the armhole as the size gets larger. This option was not available for this design, since the slant is not variable but dictated by the stitch pattern. Nevertheless, because of the openwork, stretchy fabric, the two sizes given work over a very large range of bodies.

I was especially enamored with the big fans and the fact that the garment required a mere 21 rows of crochet! Before sewing the pieces together, I played with them at the mirror as I always do and noticed that the front and back pieces could easily become sleeves.

The next thing I knew, I was designing a shrug using the same yarn in another color! The two main pieces are almost identical to the front and back pieces of the vest but now served as sleeves. There are minor variations: the sleeves have one row less of border and have a decrease at the top to fit the shoulder, as opposed to the chest on the vest. The back of the shrug is a replica of the top of the vest. For the front of the shrug, I was inspired by the diagonal lines in the pattern to make the two front pieces begin far apart and angle in to meet and overlap at the center. All this complex shaping made it impractical to offer multiple sizing for the shrug, but like the vest, it can be worn by a range of body types.

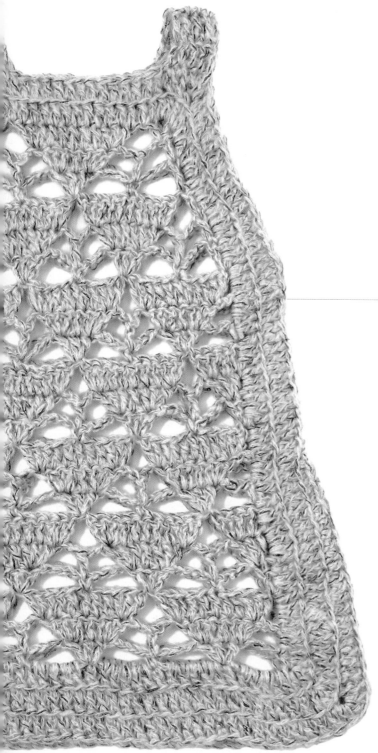

BIG FANS vest

skill level: intermediate

size

Small (Large)

finished measurements

Chest, 35 (44)"
Width at bottom, 39 (48)"
Length from shoulder, 26"

materials

Tahki Stacey Charles Loop-d-Loop Shale,
   (1.75 ounces/73 yards, 50 grams/66 meters per ball):
   #004 White/Black — 6 (7) balls
Size K-10.5 (6.5 mm) crochet hook or size needed to
   obtain gauge
I-9 (5.5 mm) or J-10 (6.00 mm) crochet hook for
   neckline edging
2 sew-on snaps, dark sewing thread and needle

gauge

2 patt reps and 6 rows: 9" x 5½"
1 border row = 1"

big fans pattern

Multiple of 12 st (add 2 ch for foundation chain)

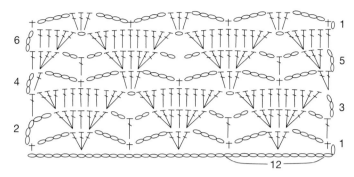

Row 1: Sc in 2nd ch from hook, *ch 4, sk 5 ch, 3 dc in next ch, ch 4, sk 5 ch, sc in next ch, rep from * across, turn.

Row 2: Ch 5 (for dc and ch 2), *sk ch 4, 3 dc in next dc, dc in next dc, 3 dc in next dc, ch 2, sk ch-4, dc in sc, ch 2, rep from * across ending dc in last sc, turn.

Row 3: Ch 3 (counts as 1st dc, ch 1), *3 dc in first dc of fan, dc in each of next 5 dc, 3 dc in last dc of fan, ch 1, sk (ch 2, dc, ch 2); rep from * ending with a completed fan, do not ch 1, dc in 3rd ch of ch 5, turn.

Row 4: Ch 3, dc in first dc, *ch 4, sk 5 dc, sc in next dc, sk 5 dc, ch 4, 3 dc in ch 1, rep from * across, ending 2 dc in tch, turn.

Row 5: Ch 3, 3 dc in 2nd dc, *ch 2, sk ch 4, dc in sc, ch 2, sk ch 4, 3 dc in next dc, dc in next dc, 3 dc in next dc, rep from * across, ending 3 dc in last dc, dc in tch, turn.

Row 6: Ch 3, dc in 2nd dc, dc in next dc, 3 dc in next dc, *ch 1, sk (ch 2, dc, ch 2); 3 dc in next dc, dc in each of next 5 dc, 3 dc in last dc of fan, rep from * across to within last 4 dc, sk (ch 2, dc, ch 2), 3 dc in next dc, dc in ea of next 2 dc, dc in tch, turn.

Row 7: Ch 1, sc in first dc, *ch 4, sk 5 dc, 3 dc in ch 1, ch 4, sk 5 dc, sc in next dc, rep from * across, ending sc in tch, turn.

Rep rows 2–7 for patt.

instructions

Vest (Make 2)

Ch 38 (50).
Work 16 rows in Big Fans pattern ending with row 4, turn — 37 (49) sts.

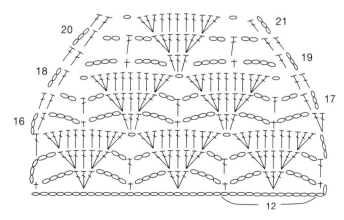

Armhole Shaping

Row 17: Ch 3, dc in 2nd dc, *ch 2, sk ch 4, dc in sc, ch 2, sk ch 4, 3 dc in next dc, dc in next dc, 3 dc in next dc, rep from * across, ending dc in last dc, dc in tch, turn — 33 (45) sts.

Row 18: Ch 3, dc in 2nd dc, *ch 1, sk (ch 2, dc, ch 2); 3 dc in next dc, dc in each of next 5 dc, 3 dc in last dc of fan, rep from * across ending ch 1, sk (ch 2, dc, ch 2), dc in next dc, dc in tch, turn.

Row 19: Ch 3, dc in 2nd dc, *ch 4, sc in 6th dc, ch 4, sk 5 dc, 3 dc in sc, rep from * ending dc in next dc, dc in tch, turn.

Row 20: Ch 3, dc in 2nd dc, *ch 2, sk ch 4, dc in sc, ch 2, sk ch 4, 3 dc in next dc, dc in next dc, 3 dc in next dc; rep from * ending ch 2, sk ch 4, dc in sc, ch 2, dc in next dc, dc in tch, turn.

Row 21: Ch 3, dc in 2nd dc, ch 1, sk (ch 2, dc, ch 2), 3 dc in next dc, dc in each of the next 5 dc, 3 dc in last dc of fan; rep from * ending ch 1, sk (ch 2, dc, ch 2), dc in next dc, dc in tch. Do not end off. Turn work 90 degrees.

Border

Work evenly spaced dc, working stitches around the tch or dc so that the original sts are not showing, as follows:

Rnd 1: Ch 3 (counts as corner st) 3 dc into each dc (counting any ch-3 as dc) 1 dc into each sc, for a total of 56 sts along side. Along bottom work 5 dc in each ch-5 sp, 1 dc in each st [35 (56) sts], 3 dc in corner st. Work 2nd side same as first (56 sts), then work 3 dc in next corner st. At top edge, dc in ea st across, sl st to top of tch.

Rnd 2: Ch 3, working into BL, work another round of dc, placing 3 dc in ea corner, sl st to top of ch 3. On one piece, end off, on the other, which will be Front, turn. Ch 3. Place loop on safety pin.

Side Gussets

Work on both sides of front and back.

With RS facing, count 21 sts up from bottom left corner, tie on, ch 1. Working into BL, sc in each of next 4 dc, hdc in ea of next 5 sts, dc in ea of next 11 dc, 3 dc in corner st, dc in ea st along bottom, 3 dc in next corner, dc in ea of next 11 dc, hdc in ea of next 5 dc, sc in ea of next 4 dc, sl st into next dc. End off.

Shoulder Strap

Pick up loop on safety pin. Dc into ea of next 4 dc, turn, ch 3. Work 3 (4) more rows of 5 dc. Attach to back by placing RS of front and back together, work sl st seam across 5 st on back. Tie on at front 5 st from corner, ch 3, dc in ea of next 4 dc, turn, ch 3. Work 3 (4) more rows of 5 dc, attach to back in same way.

finishing

RS of pieces have border showing fronts of stitches. Sew side seams on front and back together up to slant where armhole begins. Sew from RS with mattress stitch, picking up inner strand of each edge.

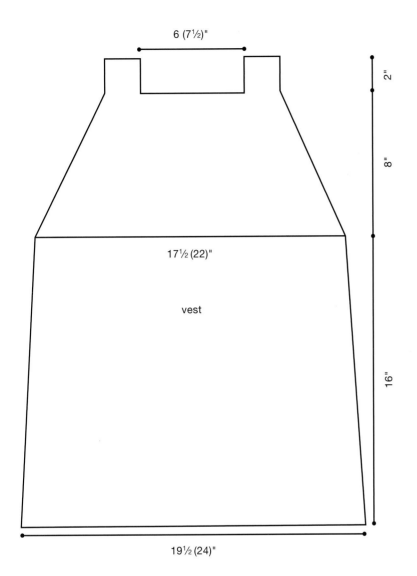

6 (7½)"

2"

8"

17½ (22)"

vest

16"

19½ (24)"

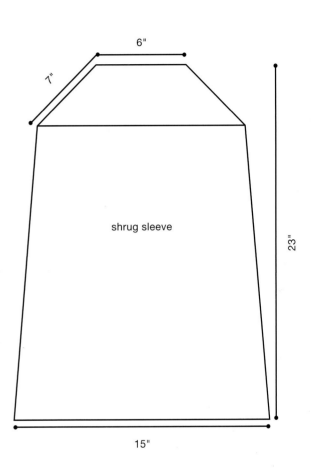

6"

7"

shrug sleeve

23"

15"

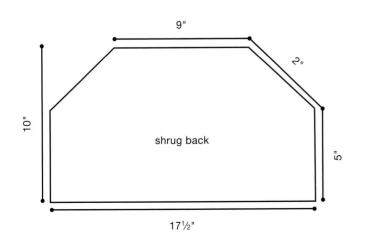

9"

2"

10"

shrug back

5"

17½"

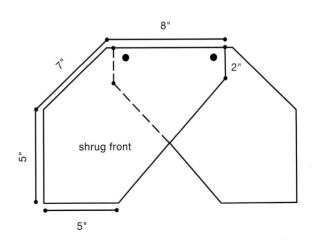

8"

7"

2"

5"

shrug front

5"

BIG FANS shrug

skill level: experienced

size
Small–Medium

finished measurements
Chest/Bust 35"

materials

Tahki Stacey Charles Loop-d-Loop Shale,
    (1.75 ounces/73 yards, 50 grams/ 66 meters
    per ball): #4 Plum — 8 balls
Size K-10.5 (6.5 mm) crochet hook
Size I-9 (5.5 mm) or J-10 (6.00 mm) crochet hook
    for neckline edging
2 sew-on snaps
Dark sewing thread and needle

gauge
2 patt reps and 6 rows: 9" x 5½"
Each border row adds 1"

big fans pattern

(See pattern on page 39)

instructions

Multiple of 12 st (add 2 ch for foundation chain)

Row 1: Sc in 2nd ch from hook, *ch 4, sk 5 ch, 3 dc in next ch, ch 4, sk 5 ch, sc in next ch, rep from * across, turn.

Row 2: Ch 5 (for dc and ch 2), *sk ch 4, 3 dc in next dc, dc in next dc, 3 dc in next dc, ch 2, sk ch-4, dc in sc, ch 2, rep from * across ending dc in last sc, turn.

Row 3: Ch 3 (counts as 1st dc, ch 1), *3 dc in first dc of fan, dc in each of next 5 dc, 3 dc in last dc of fan, ch 1, sk (ch 2, dc, ch 2); rep from * ending with a completed fan, do not ch 1, dc in 3rd ch of ch 5, turn.

Row 4: Ch 3, dc in first dc, *ch 4, sk 5 dc, sc in next dc, sk 5 dc, ch 4, 3 dc in ch 1, rep from * across, ending 2 dc in tch, turn.

Row 5: Ch 3, 3 dc in 2nd dc, *ch 2, sk ch 4, dc in sc, ch 2, sk ch 4, 3 dc in next dc, dc in next dc, 3 dc in next dc, rep from * across, ending 3 dc in last dc, dc in tch, turn.

Row 6: Ch 3, dc in 2nd dc, dc in next dc, 3 dc in next dc, *ch 1, sk (ch 2, dc, ch 2); 3 dc in next dc, dc in each of next 5 dc, 3 dc in last dc of fan, rep from * across to within last 4 dc, sk (ch 2, dc, ch 2), 3 dc in next dc, dc in ea of next 2 dc, dc in tch, turn.

Row 7: Ch 1, sc in first dc, *ch 4, sk 5 dc, 3 dc in ch 1, ch 4, sk 5 dc, sc in next dc, rep from * across, ending sc in tch, turn.

Rep rows 2–7 for patt.

Sleeve (Make 2)

Ch 38, work 16 rows in Big Fans Pattern ending with row 4, turn — 37 sts.

Armhole Shaping

Row 17: Ch 3, dc in 2nd dc, *ch 2, sk ch 4, dc in sc, ch 2, sk ch 4, 3 dc in next dc, dc in next dc, 3 dc in next dc, rep from * across, ending dc in last dc, dc in tch, turn — 33 sts.

Row 18: Ch 3, dc in 2nd dc, *ch 1, sk (ch 2, dc, ch 2); 3 dc in next dc, dc in each of next 5 dc, 3 dc in last dc of fan, rep from * across ending ch 1, sk (ch 2, dc, ch 2), dc in next dc, dc in tch, turn.

Row 19: Ch 3, dc in 2nd dc, *ch 4, sc in 6th dc, ch 4, sk 5 dc, 3 dc in sc, rep from * ending dc in next dc, dc in tch, turn.

Row 20: Ch 3, dc in 2nd dc, *ch 2, sk (ch 4, dc in sc, ch 2, sk ch 4), 3 dc in next dc, dc in next dc, 3 dc in next dc; rep from * ch 2, sk (ch 4, dc in sc, ch 2, sk 4), dc in next dc, dc in tch, turn.

Row 21: Ch 3, dc in 2nd dc, ch 1, sk (ch 2, dc, ch 2), 3 dc in next dc, dc in each of the next 5 dc, 3 dc in last dc of fan; rep from *, ch 1, sk (ch 2, dc, ch 2), dc in next dc, dc in tch. Do not end off. Turn work 90 degrees.

Sleeve Border

Work evenly spaced dc, working stitches around the tch or dc so that the original sts are not showing, as follows:

Rnd 1: Ch 3 (counts as first corner st), 3 dc into each dc (counting any tch as dc, 1 dc into each sc for a total of 56 sts along side. Along bottom work 5 dc in each ch-5 sp, 1 dc in each st [35, (56)] sts, 3 dc in corner st. Work 2nd side same as first (56 sts), then work 3 dc in next corner st. At top of sleeve, dc in ea st to center 3 st, dc3tog, dc in ea st to end, 2 dc in last corner, sl st to top of tch.

Rnd 2: Ch 3, working into BL, work another round of dc, placing 3 dc in ea corner, sl st to top of ch 3. End off.

Back

Ch 38.

Rows 1–4: Rep Big Fan Pattern, rows 1–4 — 37 sts.

Row 5: Ch 3, dc in 2nd dc, *ch 2, sk ch 4, dc in sc, ch 2, sk ch 4, 3 dc in next dc, dc in next dc, 3 dc in next dc, rep from * across, ending dc in last dc, dc in tch, turn — 33 sts.

Row 6: Ch 3, dc in 2nd dc, *ch 1, sk (ch 2, dc, ch 2); 3 dc in next dc, dc in each of next 5 dc, 3 dc in last dc of fan, rep from * across ending ch 1, sk (ch 2, dc, ch 2), dc in next dc, dc in tch, turn.

Row 7: Ch 3, dc in 2nd dc, *ch 4, sc in 6th dc, ch 4, sk 5 dc, 3 dc in sc, rep from * ending dc in next dc, dc in tch, turn.

Row 8: Ch 3, dc in 2nd dc, *ch 2, sk (ch 4, dc in sc, ch 2, sk ch 4), 3 dc in next dc, dc in next dc, 3 dc in next dc; rep from * ch 2, sk (ch 4, dc in sc, ch 2, sk 4), dc in next dc, dc in tch, turn.

Row 9: Ch 3, dc in 2nd dc, ch 1, sk (ch 2, dc, ch 2), 3 dc in next dc, dc in each of the next 5 dc, 3 dc in last dc of fan; rep from *, ch 1, sk (ch 2, dc, ch 2), dc in next dc, dc in tch. Do not end off. Turn work 90 degrees.

Back Border

Work evenly spaced dc, working stitches around the tch or dc so that the original sts are not showing, as follows:

Rnd 1: Ch 3 (counts as corner st), 3 dc into each dc (counting any ch-3 as dc), 1 dc into each sc, for a total of 24 st along side. Along bottom work 5 dc in each ch-5 sp, 1 dc in each st (35 sts) 3 dc in corner st. Work 2nd side same as first (24 sts), then work 3 dc in next corner st. At top edge, dc in ea each st across (15 sts), 2 dc in last corner st, sl st to top of tch.

Rnd 2: Ch 3, working into BL, work another round of dc, placing 3 dc in ea corner, sl st to top of tch. End off.

Front Right

Ch 8, turn.

Row 1: Sc in 2nd ch from hook, ch 4, sk 5, 3 dc in last ch, turn.

Row 2: Ch 3, 2 dc in first dc, dc in next dc, 3 dc in next dc, ch 2, dc in sc, turn.

Row 3: Ch 3, sk 2 ch, 3 dc in next dc, dc in each of next 5 dc, 3 dc in tch, turn.

Row 4: Ch 4, 2 dc in 4th ch, ch 4, sk 5 dc, sc in 6th dc of fan, ch 4, sk 5 dc, 2 dc in tch, turn.

Row 5: Ch 3, dc in 2nd dc, ch 2, sk 4, dc in sc, ch 2, sk 4, 3 dc in next dc, dc in next dc, 3 dc in tch, turn.

Row 6: Ch 3, 3 dc in first dc (1 extra stitch to stand in for ch 1), dc in each of next 5 dc, 3 dc in next dc, ch 1, sk (ch 2, dc, ch 2), dc in next dc, dc in tch, turn.

Row 7: Ch 3, dc in 2nd dc, ch 4, sk 5, sc in 6th dc of fan, ch 4, sk 5 DC, 3 dc in next dc, turn.

Row 8: Ch 3, 2 dc in first dc, dc in next dc, 3 dc in next dc, ch 2, sk 2 ch , dc in sc, ch 2, sk 2 ch, dc in next dc, dc in tch, turn.

Row 9: Ch 3, dc in 2nd dc, ch 1, sk (ch 2, dc, ch 2), 3 dc in next dc, dc in each of next 5 dc, 3 dc in tch, turn.

Front Right Border

Row 1: Dc in each st across (14 sts) 3 sts in corner st; work along side as on back, 3 dc in corner st, 5 dc along bottom ch-5, dc in base of fan, ch 1, work sc along diagonal edge in same manner as dc border, including tch at top of this edge.

Row 2: Ch 3, BL dc in each st around with 3 sts at corners, continue border along bottom edge, dc in dc that has sc border worked around it, ch 1, 2 sc in side of dc just made, sl st to sc. End off.

Front Left

Ch 10.

Row 1: 2 dc in 4th ch from hook, ch 4, sk 5 ch, sc in last ch, turn.

Row 2: Ch 5, 3 dc in first dc, dc in next dc, 3 dc in top of tch, turn.

Row 3: Ch 3, 3 dc in first dc, dc in each of next 5 dc, 3 dc in last dc of fan, dc in 3rd ch of ch 5, ch 3, turn.

Row 4: dc in 2nd dc, ch 4, sc in center dc of fan, ch 4, 3 dc in top of tch, turn.

Row 5: Ch 3, 2 dc in first dc, dc in next dc, 3 dc in next dc, ch 2, dc in sc, ch 2, dc in last dc, dc in tch, turn.

Row 6: Ch 3, dc in 2nd dc, ch 1, sk next (ch 2, dc, ch 2), dc in next dc, dc in each of the next 5 dc, 3 dc in tch, turn.

Row 7: Ch 3, 2 dc in first dc, ch 4, sk 4 dc, sc in next dc, ch 4, sk 4 dc, dc in next dc, dc in tch, turn.

Row 8: Ch 3, dc in 2nd dc, ch 2, dc in sc, ch 2, 3 dc in next dc, dc in next dc, 3 dc in tch, turn.

Row 9: Ch 3, 2 dc in first dc, dc in each of the next 5 dc, 3 dc in last dc of fan, sk next (ch 2, dc, ch 2), ch 1, dc in next dc, dc in tch, end off.

Front Left Border

With RS facing, tie on at base of foundation chain under fan at left edge, ch 3. Work dc border as on front around 3 sides of piece, end off. Tie on at top of starting ch 3 of border, work second row of border in BL as before, ch 3, turn work 90 degrees, work sc edging along diagonal edge all the way to bottom.

finishing

This piece should fit a great range of bodies. Before completing this final step, try on the shrug and determine how much tighter it needs to be to fit around shoulders. If it is fine as is, make the edging looser using a larger hook. The model is a small and was done with an I-9 hook and tight stitches. With RS facing, tie on at seam connecting right front piece to sleeve, work sl st from this point all around top of sleeve, back neckline and top of left sleeve, ending at seam on opposite side. Do not work over front pieces. RS of pieces have border showing fronts of stitches.

To sew front and back pieces to sleeves, match beginning of slant on both pieces (row 4 of back) and begin seam at this end. At top, back and front pieces exceed length of sleeve by 1 row of border (about 1"); sew this extra fabric to rounded corner at top of sleeve. Sew from RS with mattress stitch, picking up inner strand of ea edge.

Front pieces should overlap at top. Use dark thread to sew snaps to inside of upside-down triangle on right and left points to close securely.

TOREADOR JACKET

One of the first yarns I became enamored with was Lopi Lite, whose virtues include a lofty airiness and fabulous color choices. For ages, many balls of Lopi Lite lay unused in my stash, waiting for the right inspiration. What finally got the creative juices flowing was my need for something cute to show off at a Crochet Guild of America conference. The result was this quirky little jacket. It uses three colors, two stitch patterns — one closed, one open — and is put together in an unconventional manner.

Traditional sweater construction consists of separate pieces for front, back, and sleeves which are seamed together. Here, I started with a main piece that runs all around the body up to the chest. To shape the bodice, I varied the number of stitches used in the shells. This is a good, organic shaping technique that molds to the body better than the usual shaping at the sides. The yoke section is made in two pieces, each worked vertically, beginning at the center back and worked out to the end of each sleeve. This allows the stitch patterns to run in two different directions, horizontal and vertical, an effect that's one of my favorites (also used in the Caribe Coverup on page 116).

The yoke pieces run vertically over the shoulder, and yield to the lace pattern before the shoulder edge to create a figure-flattering outline in the solid section. Lace sleeves on a solid body can sometimes look strange, but I think starting the lace before the shoulders and having the pattern echoed on the bottom, integrates the lace in this design.

I remember working on this project quite feverishly to have it ready in time. Once at the conference, when the dinner event arrived, my buddy Doris Chan asked if I would model her fabulous skirt. I couldn't say no; it was absolutely gorgeous, but it didn't match my jacket. Doris and I made a deal: we wore each others' clothes and introduced them together at the dinner. I love the spirit of camaraderie among crochet designers that allows things like that to happen!

TOREADOR JACKET

skill level: intermediate

sizes

Small (Medium, Large)

finished measurements

Bust, 29 (33½, 38)" (does not close in front)
Back, 17 (19¼, 21½)"
Length from shoulder to bottom, 19 (19, 21)"

materials

Reynolds Lopi Lite 100% wool, 50g, 109 yds:
    Green (A) — ½ ball
    Mauve (B) — ½ ball
    Cranberry (MC) — 3 balls
Size I-9 (5.5 mm) crochet hook

gauge

1 patt rep = 2¼"; 4 rows in patt = 2"
For gauge swatch: Ch 36, work rows 1–4 in patt;
measure gauge on center patt reps, from left
edge of sc to left edge of next sc in row 2.

instructions

Starting at Bottom Edge

With A ch 113 (129, 145).

Row 1: Sc in 2nd ch, ch 1, sk next ch, *sc in next ch, ch 3, sk 3 ch, rep from * across to within last 3 ch, sc in next ch, ch 1, sk next ch, sc in last ch, change to B, turn — 14 (16, 18) patt reps.

Row 2: Ch 1, sc in first sc, ch 1, sk ch-1 sp and sc, *6 dc in ch-3 sp, ch 1, sc in next ch-3 sp, ch 1, rep from * to last 3 sts, sk 2nd to last sc and ch-1 sp, ch 1, sc in last sc, turn.

Row 3: Ch 1, sc in first sc, *sc in ch 1 sp, (ch 2, sk 2 dc, sc between next 2 dc) 2 times, ch 2, sc in ch-1 sp, ch 1, rep from * across, on last rep do not ch 1, sc in last sc, change to A, turn.

Row 4: Ch 3, dc in first sc, ch 2, *sk (sc, ch 2, sc) 2 dc in next ch-2 sp, ch 2, sk (sc, ch 2, sc), 2 dc in ch-1 sp, ch 2, rep from * across, to last 4 st, ch 2, 2 dc in last sc, turn — 29 (31, 33) pairs of dc.

Row 5: Ch 1, sc in first dc, ch 1, sc in ch-2 sp, *ch 3, sk 2 dc, sc in ch-2 sp, rep from * across, ending ch 1, sc in tch, change to B, turn.

Waist Shaping

Row: 6: Ch 3, dc in ch-1 sp, *ch 1, sc in ch-3 sp, ch 1, 6 dc in ch-3 sp, ch 1, sc in ch 3 sp, ch 1, 5 dc in ch 3 sp, rep from * across, ending sc in last ch-3 sp, ch 1, dc in last ch-1 sp, dc in last sc, turn.

Row 7: Ch 1, sc in first dc, sk next dc, ch 1 *sc in ch-1 sp, ch 1, sc in ch-1 sp (ch 2, sk 2 dc, sc between next 2 dc) two times, ch 2, sc in ch-1 sp, ch 1, sc in ch-1 sp, ch 2, sk 2 dc, sc in next dc, ch 2, sk 2 dc, rep from * across, ending sc in ch-1 sp, sk dc, ch 1, sc in tch, change to A, turn.

Row 8: Ch 4 (counts as dc and ch 1), sk (ch-1 sp, sc), 2 dc in next ch-1 sp, *ch 3, sk next ch-2 sp, 2 dc in next ch-2 sp, ch 3, sk next ch-2 sp, 2 dc in ch-1 sp, ch 3, sk ch-2 sp, dc in next sc, ch 3, sk next ch-2 sp, 2 dc in next ch-1 sp, rep from * across, ending ch 1, dc in last sc, turn.

Row 9: Ch 1, sc in dc, *ch 3, sc in next ch-3 sp, rep from * across, ending sc in 3rd ch of tch, change to MC, turn.

Row 10: Ch 3, 3 dc in ch-3 sp, *sc in next ch-3 sp, 6 dc in next ch-3 sp, rep from * across to last ch-3 sp, 3 dc in last ch-3 sp, dc in last sc, turn — 13 (15, 17) patt reps.

Row 11: Ch 1, sc in first dc, *6 dc in next sc, sk 2 dc, sc between next 2 dc, rep from * across, ending sc in last dc, turn.

Row 12: Ch 3, 2 dc in sc,* sk 2 dc, sc between next 2 dc, 6 dc in next sc, rep from * across, ending 3 dc in last sc, turn.

Row 13: Ch 1, sc in first dc, *5 dc in next sc, sk 2 dc, sc between next 2 dc, rep from * across, ending sc in tch, turn.

Row 14: Ch 3, 2 dc in first sc, *sc in 3rd dc of fan, 5 dc in sc, rep from * across, ending 3 dc in last sc, turn.

Bust Shaping

Row 15: Ch 1, sc in first dc, 6 dc in next sc, sk 2 dc, sc in 3rd dc of fan, rep from * across, ending sc in tch, turn.

Row 16: Rep row 12.

Row 17: Rep row 13.

Row 18: Ch 3, 3 dc in first sc, *sc in 3rd dc of fan, 7 dc in sc, rep from * across, ending 4 dc in last sc, turn.

Row 19: Ch 1, sc in first dc, *7 dc in next sc, sk 3 dc, sc in next dc, rep from * across, ending sc in tch, turn.

Row 20: Ch 3, 3 dc in first sc, *sc in 4th dc of fan, 7 dc in next sc, rep from * across, ending sc in tch, end off.

Note: If you wish to make a longer garment, add additional reps of rows 19 and 20 (2 rows add 1½" to length).

Yoke and Sleeve (Make 2)

Note: These pieces begin at the center back and work out to the sleeve. After row 3, odd rows start at front and even rows start at back.

With MC, Ch 26 (8 x 3 + 2).

Row 1: Sc in 2nd ch and in each ch across, turn — 25 (25, 33) sc.

Row 2: Ch 1, sc in first sc, sk 3 sc, *7 dc in next sc, sk 3 sc, sc in next sc, rep from * across, ch 56 (56, 64), turn — 3 patt reps.

Row 3: Ch 3, 3 dc in 4th ch from hook, *sk 3 ch, sc in next ch, sk 3 ch, 7 dc in next ch, rep from * over added remaining chains, then continue in patt over stitches in row 2 ending with 4 dc in last sc, turn — 10 (10, 12) patt reps.

Row 4: Ch 1, sc in first dc, *6 dc in next sc, sk 3 dc, sc in next dc, sk 3 dc, rep from * across, ending with sc in tch, turn.

Row 5: Ch 3, 2 dc in sc, sk 2 dc, sc between next 2 dc, sk 3 dc, *6 dc in next sc, sk 2 dc, sc between next 2 dc, sk 3 dc, rep from * across, ending 3 dc in last sc, turn.

Rows 6–7 (6–9, 6–11): Rep rows 4 & 5.

Row 8 (10, 12): Ch 1, sc in first dc, *5 dc in next sc, sk 2 dc, sc in 3rd dc of fan, sk 2 dc, rep from * across, ending 5 dc in next sc, sk 2 dc, sc in tch, turn.

Row 9 (11, 13): Ch 3, 2 dc in first sc, *sk 2 dc, sc in 3rd dc of fan, sk 2 dc, 5 dc in sc, rep from * across, ending with sk 2 dc, sc in 3rd dc of fan, sk 2 dc, 3 dc in last sc, turn.

Row 10 (12, 14): Rep row 8, change to A, turn.

Row 11 (13, 15): Ch 5, sk 2 dc, *2 dc in next dc, ch 2, sk 2 dc**, dc in sc, ch 2, rep from * across, ending last rep at ** dc in last sc, turn.

Row 12 (14, 16): Ch 1, sc in dc, ch 3, sk (ch-2, 2 dc), *sc in next ch-2 sp, ch 3, sk dc, sc in next ch-2 sp, ch 3, sk 2 dc, rep from * across ending sc in 3rd ch of tch, change to B, turn.

Row 13 (15, 17): Ch 1, sc in sc, ch 1, *4 dc in ch-3 sp, ch 1, sk sc, sc in next ch-3 sp, ch 1, sk sc, rep from * across, ending 4 dc in last ch-3 sp, ch 1, sc in last sc, turn.

Row 14 (16, 18): Ch 1, sc in sc, *ch 2, sk 2 dc, sc between next 2 dc, ch 2, sk 2 dc**, sc in ch-1 sp, ch 1, sk sc, sc in next ch-1 sp, rep from * across, ending last rep at ** sc in last sc, change to A, turn.

Row 15 (17, 19): Ch 5, *dc in sc, ch 2, sk (ch 2, sc) 2 dc in ch-1 sp, ch 2, sk (sc, ch 2), rep from * across ending dc in sc, sk (sc, 2 ch), dc in last sc, turn.

Row 16 (18, 20): Ch 1, sc in dc, *sc in ch-2 sp, ch 3, rep from * across ending sc in ch-5 sp, sc in 3rd ch of tch, change to B, turn.

Row 17 (19, 21): Ch 4, sk sc, *sc in ch-3 sp, ch 1, 4 dc in ch-3 sp, ch 1, rep from * across, ending sc in last ch-3 sp, ch 1, sk sc, dc in last sc, turn.

Row 18 (20, 22): Ch 1, sc in dc, *sc in ch-1 sp, ch-1, sc in next ch-1 sp, ch 2, sk 1 dc, sc between next 2 dc, ch-2, sk 2 dc, rep from * across to last 4 st, sc in ch-1 sp, ch 1, sc in last ch-1 sp, sc in tch, change to A, turn.

Row 19 (21, 23): Decrease row (to shape sleeves): Ch 3, sk sc, *2 dc in ch-1 sp, ch 2, sk (sc, ch 2), dc in sc, ch 2, sk (ch 2, sc) rep from * ending with 2 dc in last ch-1 sp, sk sc, dc in last sc, ch 1, turn (minus 6 sts).

Row 20 (22, 24): Ch 1, sk dc, sc in next dc, sk dc, *sc in ch-2 sp, ch 3, rep from * across ending sc in last ch-2 sp, sk dc, sc in last dc, change to B, turn.

Row 21 (23, 25): Decrease row. Ch 3, dc in sc, ch 1, sk sc, *sc in ch-3 sp, ch 1, sk sc, 4 dc in ch-3 sp, ch 1, sk sc, rep from * across, ending sc in last ch-3 sp, ch 1, sk sc, 2 dc in last sc, turn (minus 4 st).

Row 22 (24, 26): Ch 1, sc in dc, sk dc, *sc in ch-1 sp, ch 1, sk sc, sc in ch-1 sp, ch 2, sk 1 dc, sc between next 2 dc, sk 2 dc, ch 2, rep from * across, ending sc in next ch-1 sp, ch 1, sk sc, sc in next ch-1 sp, sc in last dc, change to A, turn.

Row 23 (25, 27): Ch 3, sk sc, *2 dc in ch-1 sp, ch 2, sk (sc, ch 2) dc in sc, ch 2, sk (ch 2, sc), rep from * across, ending 2 dc in last ch-1 sp, sk sc, dc in last sc, turn (minus 4 sts).

Row 24 (26, 28): Ch 1, sc in dc, sk dc, sc in ch-1 sp, *ch 3, sc in ch-2 sp, rep from * across, ending sc in last dc, change to B, turn.

Row 25 (27, 29): Ch 3, dc in sc, *ch 1, sk sc, sc in ch-3 sp, ch 1, sk sc, 4 dc in ch-3 sp, rep from * across, ending ch 1, sk sc, sc in last ch-3 sp, ch 1, 2 dc in last sc, turn.

Row 26 (28, 30): Ch 1, sc in dc, ch 1, sk dc, *sc in ch-1 sp, ch 1, sk sc, sc in ch-1 sp, ch 2, sk 1 dc, sc between next 2 dc, sk 2 dc, ch 2, rep from * across, ending sc in next ch-1 sp, ch 1, sk sc, sc in last ch-1 sp, ch 1, sk dc, sc in tch, change to A, turn.

Row 27 (29, 31): Ch 5, sk (ch-1, sc), *2 dc in ch-1 sp, ch 2, sk (sc, ch 2) dc in sc, ch 2, sk (ch 2, sc), rep from * ending 2 dc in ch-1 sp, ch 2, sk (sc, ch 1), dc in last sc, turn.

Row 28 (30, 32): Ch 1, sc in dc, *sc in ch-2 sp, ch 3, rep from * across ending sc in ch-5 sp, sc in 3rd ch of tch, end off.

finishing

Sew together the 2 yoke pieces at the center back. On main body piece, at top edge, count 7 (8, 9) patt reps from either side to find center point and mark this point with safety pin or stitch marker.

Step 1: Line up seam of yoke piece to this point and pin section of yoke using MC only.

Step 2: Take the sides of the main body and fold inward toward the center. This will be the front edges of the jacket.

Step 3: Fold down the opposite end of the yoke to meet the front edges on both sides. Beginning with center edges, pin the front yoke to the body. Pin the MC section, then continue pinning using as many rows as necessary of openwork, 2-color section until you reach the side of the garment. Do this on both sides of front.

Step 4: Carefully turn the garment over. Finish pinning the back yoke seam, using the same number of rows of openwork section, until you meet the other piece at the garment's side. Do this on both sides. Sew this seam all around from WS. Sew sleeve seams.

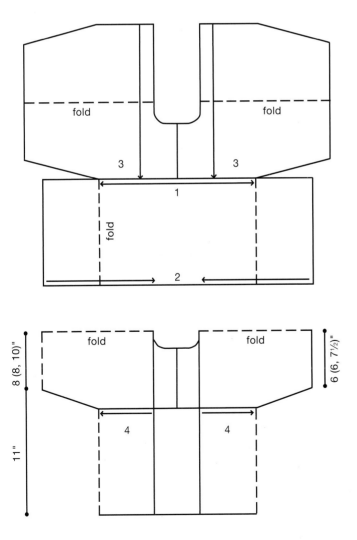

chapter two DIAMONDS AND WHEELS

projects GOTTA RUANA
LUX-LOOK SCARF
PEACHES & CREAM BELT
A ROSE IS A ROSE JACKET
DIAMOND HEADS PINK
DIAMOND HEADS BLUE
PRECIOSILLA PURSE

What can I say about falling in love with diamonds and wheels? I lay the beginning of this obsession at the feet of the great designer Sylvia Cosh. Thumbing through my treasured copy of *The Crochet Sweater Book* (1987), I always linger on those gorgeous designs where she combines diamonds with color work, painting with yarn like a master. I find it fascinating that now, over 20 years later, yarn companies are developing variegated yarns with long, random repeats of color, aiming at a very similar look. On the one hand, it saves the crafter from cutting a multitude of yarn ends; on other, what an adventure it was to work Sylvia's way, combining 14 subtly different yarns in a design.

When I first got into designing, eyelash and other textured yarns were all the rage, and I was constantly on the lookout for stitch patterns that would remain visible even if individual stitches were not. Wheels and diamonds are very reliable that way, and I think of them as bold graphic stitch patterns which ensure "pattern definition," as opposed to stitch definition. Since the latter is lost with highly textured yarns, I often use a bold graphic pattern to supply this visual element in a design.

I also enjoy the architecture of these stitch patterns, the clustering of stitches that creates right-side-up and upside-down fans, the way one row builds on another, and how the rows interlock. The main difference between Diamonds and Wheels, as they are shown in most stitch dictionaries, is that the latter has fewer double crochet stitches and more single crochets between the wheels. Of course, one can create variations on these two examples, as I have in this chapter. Have I exhausted my passion for these stitches with the seven designs shown here? I doubt it!

stitching tips

TIP 1. Multiple stitches in the foundation chain

When working many stitches into a foundation chain, it's likely that some of the adjacent chains will be covered by the multiple stitches. In order to be sure you are skipping 3 chains as instructed in the first row of this pattern, give a tug on the foundation chain to pull out any chains covered by the 9 double crochet stitches.

There are different ways of working into the foundation chain. I generally work into the back loop only, and I know some who are devoted to the technique of working into the bump at the back of the chain. In a pattern like this, however, where multiple stitches are being worked into the foundation chain, neither of these methods is the best choice; a single strand will stretch out of shape and not gather the stitches effectively at the base. It's wiser to work into both loops of the chain in this case, so your stitches are nicely gathered at the base.

TIP 2. Double crochet stitches that stand tall

In many of the patterns used throughout this book, the look of your work will be improved by making the double crochet stitches tall. Begin as usual with a yarn over, insert hook in the designated stitch and pull up a loop — here's the crucial moment. Pull up this loop to a good height, about ⅜", then yarn over and complete the stitch as usual. This technique makes all cluster stitches fuller and shows off strands of yarn nicely, too.

TIP 3. Avoiding an oversized loop on the first stitch after skipping stitches

This type of stitch pattern, where several stitches are skipped, can present a pesky little problem: the loop at the top of your first stitch after skipping stitches wants to enlarge. To avoid this, bend the work to bring the stitch you're working into close to the last stitch worked, and tug a bit on the working yarn to remove any excess.

GOTTA RUANA

A simple, unshaped construction is used for this "ruana," a name I am using because it's cool and exotic and because we don't really have another for this kind of garment. Unlike the traditional Celtic Ruana, I have stitched the side seams closed. Whatever you call it, it sure is useful, and to me is more versatile and less dated than a poncho.

The lovely yarn used here, Austermann Murano, a German yarn distributed in the U.S. by Skacel, has a long repeat of each color. Amazingly, the striped effect on this ruana was not planned at all. In fact, if you look closely, you can see the color changes sometimes occur in the middle of the row.

To achieve pleasing drape with this chunky yarn, I went all the way up to a size M hook. I didn't start there, trust me: many test swatches were made with gradually larger hooks. Because the diamonds have clusters consisting of nine double crochet stitches, they tend to thicken the fabric, something I didn't realize until this experiment.

This design features a shawl collar, an element I find very attractive and fun to make. You may have already noticed that this garment is worked vertically, making the shawl collar that much easier to do, since it grows right out of the body of the front pieces. To make a shawl collar, you simply add fabric to the front lapels. They need to be long enough to meet at the center of the neck on the garment's back. So if your neckline is 7" in width, for example, you would make each extension 3½" longer. For a soft, feathery edge on the collar, I added a row of plain double crochet stitches with an even larger hook.

The ruana works well with a trendy leather or suede belt, but I also designed a crochet cord belt for it, for a more casual look.

GOTTA RUANA

skill level: intermediate

finished size

One size fits most

finished measurements

Front side width without trim, 16"
Back width, 23"
Length from shoulder, 25"
Armhole depth, 12"

materials

Austermann Murano, (5.25 ounces/252 yards, 150
   grams/230 meters per ball): #009 Gold, Purple
   Multi-color — 4 balls
Size M-13 (9 mm) or size needed to obtain gauge
Size N/P-15 (10 mm) crochet hook (for trim)
Size I-9 (5.5 mm) crochet hook for belt (optional)

gauge

2 patt reps = 6¼"
8 rows = 7"

stitching technique

Each diamond has an "eye" in the center. The eye is
the last half of the dcXtog stitch, which holds all of the
double crochets together. Work X dcs into the eye on
the next row to complete the diamond pattern.

catherine's diamond pattern

Multiple of 8 + 2

Row 1: Sc in 2nd ch from hook, *sk 3 ch, 7 dc in next st, sk 3 ch, sc in next st, rep from * to end, turn.

Row 2: Ch 3 (count as 1st dc), dc3tog over next 3 dc, *ch 3, sc in next dc, ch 3, dc7tog over (3 dc, sc, 3dc), rep from * across, ending with dc4tog over (last 3dc, sc), turn.

Row 3: Ch 3 (count as 1st dc), 3 dc into eye, *sk ch 3, sc in sc, sk ch 3, 7 dc into eye, rep from * ending last rep with 4 dc into last eye, turn.

Row 4: Ch 1, sc in first dc, *ch 3, dc7tog over (3 dc, sc, 3dc), ch 3, sc in next dc, rep from * ending last rep with sc into top of tch, turn.

Row 5: Ch 1, sc into first sc, *sk ch 3, 7 dc into eye, sk ch 3, sc into next sc, rep from * to end, turn.

Rep rows 2–5 for pattern.

instructions

Back

With hook M, ch 66.

Row 1: Work in patt for 8 reps.

Rows 2–26: Rep rows 2–5 in patt, ending on row 2.

Front (Make 2 Including Shawl Collar)

With hook M, ch 66.

Row 1: Work in patt for 8 reps.

Rows 2–10: Rep rows 2–5 in patt, ending on row 2, ch 12, turn.

Shawl Collar

Row 11: 3 dc in 4th ch from hook, *sk ch 3, sc in sc, sk ch 3, 7 dc into eye, rep from * ending last rep with 4 dc into last eye, turn — 9 patt reps.

Rows 12 & 13: Rep rows 4 & 5 in patt.

Rows 14–19: Rep rows 2–5 in patt ending on row 3, end off.

finishing

Due to the color changes in this yarn, it is advisable to sew side seams from WS, picking up inner strands. This will make seams as invisible as possible. Sew the seam from the bottom up to desired depth of armhole. Model armhole depth is 12".

Carefully pin shawl collar along back neckline so that the two halves meet at the center. Sew from WS in the same manner as side seam. Then sew the center seam of the collar itself.

Trim

Row 1: With RS facing, tie on at bottom right corner of front. Using hook N, work dc in each st along center front edge, neckline, and opposite front edge to bottom, end off.

Belt (optional)

With I-9 hook, ch 2. Sc in 2nd ch from hook, and turn work to the right. Insert hook down through lp on the left side and work sc, *turn work to the right, insert hook down through 2 lps on left side and make sc, rep from * until cord is desired length. Model is 92".

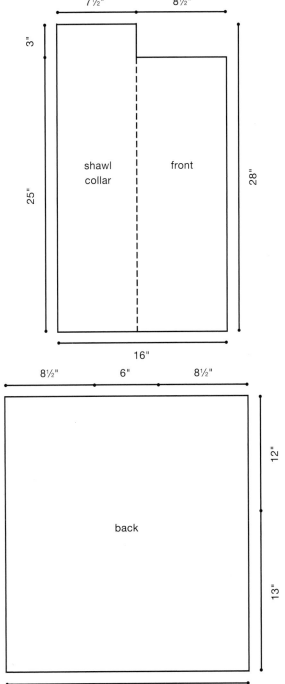

LUX-LOOK SCARF

"An interesting plainness is the most difficult thing to achieve." — Charles Eames

I often think of this quote by the famed furniture designer, and this project brought home the point to me. I wanted to use the luxurious Divine yarn by Skacel for a scarf because of its marvelous soft and silky quality, using neutral colors that can be worn with most outerwear. I swatched various ways of changing colors with this diamond wheel pattern and decided upon these staggered stripes. As the number of rows in the brown stripe is odd, not even, the grey/white stripes begin at different points in the pattern, giving them a slightly out of kilter quality.

Still, when I finished the full length of the scarf, I thought it needed a lift from the edging to get it beyond plainness. Again, I tried different ideas: rows of single crochet in different colors, crab stitch (also known as reverse single crochet) around a row of white single crochet, half doubles instead of singles. I liked the added dimension given by the crab stitch and decided to go even further by using puffs, then came upon the idea of alternating the colors. It's an effect used as trim in Chanel suits I've always admired.

When I finished adding this edging, I realized how much it changed the original concept of the scarf. Is it still plain? Is it an interesting plainness? I like to think so.

LUX-LOOK SCARF

skill level: intermediate

finished measurement

8" x 72" with border

materials

Skacel Divine (1.75 ounces/110 yards, 50 grams/100 meters
   per ball) 2 balls each of colors:
   #02 Soft Brown (A)
   #07 Off-white (B)
   #06 Grey (C)
Size H-8 (5 mm) crochet hook or size needed to obtain gauge
Size I-9 (5.5 mm) crochet hook for trim

gauge

4 rows in pattern = 7" x 3"

stitching tip

Puffs in Edging: This edging takes special attention to come out
well. It's a good way to practice distributing edging evenly when
working with a different gauge than your main work. You want to
observe how much space the puffs take up when they look best.
This might not be the same for every stitcher, since we tend to
vary in tension. I recommend working at least a foot of edging to
see how far apart you want the stitches. They should lie close together — not so close as to be crammed, but not so far apart as
to allow a visible gap between them. The tops of stitches should
be as even as possible, and the back — oh well, if there is a way
to make the back of puffs look as good as the fronts, I haven't
discovered it! It's rather easy for yarn carried at the back to slip
away, so check the back of your work often. To avoid the task of
weaving in all the ends left by color changes in the main body of
the scarf, I tried working over the unwoven ends with this edging.
It didn't work too well for me, as I could not enclose all those
loose ends neatly, so weaving in all ends first is recommended.

catherine's wheel pattern

Multiple of 10 + 1 (add 1 for foundation row)

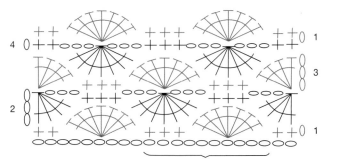

Note: Each diamond has an "eye" in the center. The eye is the last half of the dcXtog stitch, which holds all of the double crochets together. You work X dcs into the eye on the next row to complete the diamond pattern.

Row 1: Ch 1, sc in 2nd ch from hook, sc in next ch, *sk 3 ch, 7 dc in next st, sk 3 ch, sc in next 3 ch, rep from * across ending with sc in last 2 chs, turn.

Row 2: Ch 3, dc4tog over next 4 sts, *ch 3, sc in next 3 dc, ch 3, dc7tog over (dc, dc, sc, sc, sc, dc, dc), rep from * across ending with dc4tog over last (dc, dc, sc, sc), turn.

Row 3: Ch 3, 4 dc in first eye, *sk ch-3, sc in next 3 sc, sk ch-3, 7 dc in eye, rep from * across, ending with 4 dcs last eye, turn.

Row 4: Ch 1, sc in first 2 sts, *ch 3, dc7tog over (dc, dc, sc, sc, sc, dc, dc), ch 3, sc in next 3 dc, rep from * across ending with sc in last 2 sts.

Rep rows 1–4 for pattern.

Note: When changing colors, draw new color through last 2 lps on hook on final stitch before color change.

instructions

Puff Stitch with Alternating Colors: *(Yo, insert hook in designated stitch and pull up a loop) 3 times, draw second color through all 7 lps on hook. Pull gently on new color before beginning next puff to remove excess bunching of yarn at back, ch 1, rep from * to end. Carry both colors along back of work and work puff stitch around the unused strand. To avoid tangling balls of yarn, keep working yarn in front of unused yarn, moving ball back and forth as you work. Check back of work from time to time.

Scarf

With smaller hook and A, ch 32.

Row 1–114: Rep Wheel Pattern rows 1–4 following this color scheme: 1 row A, 2 rows B, 2 rows C, *6 rows A, (2 rows B, 2 rows C) 2 times, rep from * 7 times, 6 rows A, 2 rows B, 2 rows C, 1 row A.

At end of last row, change color to C, ch 2, turn work 90 degrees. Secure last loop on safety pin. Weave in all ends.

Alternating Colors Puff Border

Note: Check that RS of work is facing — diamonds have a smoother, flatter appearance on RS.

With larger hook and RS facing, working around stitches at sides of rows, work evenly spaced puffs, alternating C and B. Keep in mind the Stitching Tip on page 62 — the look of your puffs is more important than maintaining exact stitch count. Model has 4 puffs in each half diamond, 1 puff in each sc, 2 puffs in each corner, 20 puffs along shorter edges of scarf.

PEACHES &
CREAM BELT

Louet's linen yarns have been much admired in the industry, and they provide an interesting new texture for crocheters. The linen is stiffer than other yarns but softens dramatically with washing. The added body in crocheted linen fabric is perfect for a belt. This design is an example of how to use a tighter gauge to obtain a more structured piece. Two nicely blended colors are used to make a two-toned diamond, changing color at the end of each row.

The buckle for this belt is the simplest kind of closure and makes it easy for the belt to be adjustable in length. You simply wrap one end of the belt around the center post and tack it down on the inside with sewn stitches or snaps. I used snaps, which provides the option of more than one length, for wearing at either the waist or hip. To close the belt, weave the other end under and over the buckle.

There is another belt of a different character in the final chapter of this book. It is worked vertically, while this one is worked horizontally.

PEACHES & CREAM BELT

skill level: intermediate

women's sizes

Small (Medium, Large, X-large)

finished measurement

36 (39, 42, 45)"

materials

2 FINE

Louet Euroflax linen yarn (1.75 ounces/135 yards, 124 meters/50
   grams per skein):
   #01 Champagne (A) — 1 skein
   #47 Terra Cotta (B) — 1 skein
Size C-2 (2.75 mm) crochet hook or size needed to obtain gauge
Belt buckle with center post measuring approximately 1½"

Note: The belt is designed to be adjustable in length, so that it
can be worn either at the waist or hip. You may also choose to
make it a waist-only length. Measure yourself at the hip or waist,
then add 5–6" to this length for the total length to make. These
extra inches are used at either end of the belt.

For example:
36" hip, plus 6" = 42". Divide the number of inches by 1.5:
42 divided by 1.5 = 28

Round the number to the nearest whole digit — in this case 28.
That is the number of pattern repeats to make. The starting chain
is number of diamonds multiplied by 8, plus 2 for the end stitch
and the turning chain. The sizes given below are for hips; follow
the steps outlined above for a shorter, waist-size belt.The finishing instructions will explain how to make the belt fit waist or hips.

gauge

3 patt reps = 4"
4 rows = 1½"

catherine's diamond pattern

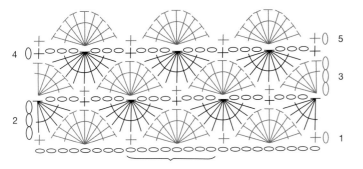

stitching tip

To review some of the stitching tips given earlier, for attractive fans that gather tightly at their base, work all the double crochet stitches under the two top lps of the foundation stitches. After making each 9-dc fan in row 1, pull on the foundation chain to expose any chains hidden under them. They will be under there, I guarantee, and you don't want to miss them or your stitch count will be off for sure.

Note: Each diamond has an "eye" in the center. The eye is the last half of the dcXtog stitch, which holds all of the double crochets together. You work X dcs into the eye on the next row to complete the diamond pattern.

Note: This yarn is stretchy, and you may want to adjust size to allow for stretch.

instructions

With A, ch 202 (226, 258, 282).

Row 1: Sc in 2nd ch from hook, *sk 3 ch, 9 dc in next ch, sk 3 ch, sc in next ch, rep from * across, change to B, ch 3, turn 25 (28, 32, 35) patt reps.

Row 2: Dc4tog over next 4 dc, ch 3, sc in next dc, *ch 3, dc9tog over (4 dc, sc, 4 dc), ch 3, sc in next dc, rep from * across ending ch 3, dc5tog over (4 dc, sc), change to A, ch 3, turn.

Row 3: 4 dc in eye, sk ch-3, sc in sc, *sk ch-3, 9 dc in eye, sk ch-3, sc in sc, rep from * across, ending sk ch-3, 5 dc in eye, change to B, ch 1, turn.

Row 4: *Sc in first dc, ch 3, dc9tog over (4dc, sc, 4 dc), ch 3, rep from * across, ending with sc in last dc.

finishing

Weave in ends. Fold one end of belt around center post of buckle. Put belt on and close it by weaving the opposite end into the buckle. Now adjust the length of the belt by pulling the folded-in edge to the appropriate length.

Pin the folded-in edge in place on WS of belt. If you plan to always wear the belt in the same place (either waist or hip), sew this end in place from WS. For more flexibility (keep in mind your diet plans!), use snaps on the inside instead.

A ROSE IS
A ROSE JACKET

My first design when returning to crochet after a 25-year hiatus used diamonds, and I intended to recreate that sweater here. To make a jacket a few years ago, I laid out a very favorite denim jacket and made a pattern with some heavy brown paper. Then I worked out the number of stitches for the bottom rows. Not knowing much about construction, I completely faked the decreases and increases for waist shaping — and this jacket was very shaped — but as it was just for myself, no one would know or care. When I was done with the back and front pieces, I liked what I had but was looking for that extra thrill. I make many design decisions by holding up swatches in front of myself in the mirror and moving the fabric pieces this way and that. This is actually the great thing about gauge swatches — they are mobile little design tools! Eventually I decided upon the idea of a flouncy collar and lapels.

Fortunately I'm now more experienced and was able to work out a way of recreating the shaping in that original design without indulging in the sort of freeform shaping used earlier. This technique is really useful for shaping with complex cluster patterns: gradually changing the number of stitches in the cluster.

Note that this jacket is worked in horizontal rows. At the bottom, where it should be wide and flouncy, I used 11 double crochets in the diamonds. As you work up to the waist, the number of stitches in the diamonds is decreased, first to 9, then to 7. In your "upside-down" rows, you need to adjust the number of chains between diamonds accordingly. Working back up to the bustline, the number is increased back to 9. It's convenient to keep the number of diamonds odd, since you need to work into the center of the diamond in the subsequent row.

Counting stitches may tax the brain a bit, but it makes for a really well-fitted shape. And the truth is, if you get off by a stitch or two here or there, not to worry (no ripping necessary). As long as you adjust the number in the next row, everything will work out fine. Just add or take away a double crochet, when necessary, to compensate for any errors.

When I got to the front of this jacket, I decided to depart from the original. Perhaps it's because every day I pass a gorgeous shop in my neighborhood that features one of a kind garments. I found myself repeatedly admiring the assymetrical front pieces in many of the designs there and decided to go for that look.

The yarn used in this design is another terrific Louet product called Gems, a 100% merino. It's a mutli-colored yarn, and when I first swatched it with diamonds, I liked the way the pattern seemed to explode from the center. The stripes in a contrasting color were added to give a bit more visual definition to the whole design. I chose half double crochet stitches for the stripes because the back of these stitches have an extra dimension I really like. Interestingly, when I first added the stripes, I worked the half doubles right into the diamonds, but the effect was not pleasing. The upside-down row of diamonds has chains between diamonds and something about the contrasting color wrapped around these chains was unattractive. That's why there is a row of single crochet stitches in the main color preceding each stripe.

In the notes for the ruana earlier in this chapter, I mentioned that the diamond pattern tends to thicken the fabric, so here again I used a larger hook than one would normally use in a worsted weight yarn. Again, as in the ruana, I used long, plain stitches for the collar, aiming for a slightly ruffled, airy look.

A ROSE IS
A ROSE JACKET

skill level: intermediate

sizes

Small–Medium (Large–1x, 2x–3x)

finished measurements

Chest, 36 (44, 51)"
Armhole, 9 (10, 12)"
Neck opening, 11 (11, 14)"
Sleeves, 17 (17, 19)"

materials

Louet Gems Merino (3.5 ounces/175 yards, 100
   grams/160 meters per skein):
   #80-2804-7 Peony (MC) — 7 (7, 8) skeins
   #80-2524-11 Grape (A) — 1 (1, 2) skeins
Size H-8 (5.5 mm) crochet hook or size needed to
   obtain gauge
1 black snap with ⅝" diameter

gauge

2 patt of 9 dc diamonds = 3.5"
4 rows of 9 dc diamonds = 3"

stitching techniques

Note: Each diamond has an "eye" in the center. The
eye is the last half of the dcXtog stitch, which holds all
of the double crochets together. Work X dcs into the
eye on the next row to complete the diamond pattern.
Refer to stitch diagram on page 67.

(see Catherine's Diamond 9-dc variation on page 67)

instructions

In all rows following an hdc row, the last st is worked into tch.

Back

With MC, ch 92 (112, 132).

Row 1: Sc in 2nd ch from hook, *sk 4 ch, 11 dc in next ch, sk 4 ch, sc in next ch rep from * across, ch 3, turn — 9 (11, 13) patt reps.

Row 2: Dc5tog over 5 dc (eye formed at center top of dc5tog), *ch 4, sc in next dc, ch 4, dc11tog over (5 dc, sc, 5 dc), rep from * across ending with ch 4, dc6tog over last (5 dc, sc), ch 3, turn.

Row 3: 5 dc in eye, *sc in sc, 11 dc in eye, rep from * across ending with 6 dc in last eye, ch 1, turn.

Row 4: Sc in first dc, *ch 4, dc11tog over (5 dc, sc, 5 dc), ch 4, sc in next dc, rep from * across ending with sc in tch, ch 1, turn.

Row 5: *Sc in sc, 11 dc in next eye, rep from * across ending with sc in last sc, ch 3, turn.

Rows 6–8: Rep rows 2–4.

Row 9: *Sc in sc, 3 sc in ch-4 sp, sc in eye, 3 sc in ch-4 sp, rep from * across ending with sc in last sc, end MC — 73 (89, 105) sc.

Row 10: With A ch 2, turn. Hdc in each sc across, hdc in tch, end A.

Row 11: With MC ch 1 turn. Sc in first hdc, *sk 3 hdc, 9 dc in next hdc, sk 3 hdc, sc in next hdc, rep from * across, ch 3, turn.

Row 12: Dc4tog over 4 dc, *ch 3, sc in next dc, ch 3, dc9tog over (4 dc, sc, 4 dc), rep from * across ending with dc5tog over (4 dc, sc), ch 3, turn.

Row 13: 4 dc in eye, * sc in sc, 9 dc in eye, rep from * across ending with 5 dc in last eye, ch 1, turn.

Row 14: Sc in first dc, *ch 3, dc9tog over (4 dc, sc, 4 dc), ch 3, sc in next dc, rep from * across ending with sc in tch, ch 1, turn.

Row 15: *Sc in sc, 9 dc in next eye, rep from * across ending with sc in last sc, ch 3, turn.

Row 16: Dc4tog over 4 dc, *ch 3, sc in next dc, ch 3, dc9tog over (4 dc, sc, 4 dc), rep from * across ending with dc5tog over (4 dc, sc), ch 1, turn.

Waist Shaping

Row 17: *Sc in eye, 2 sc in ch-3 sp, sc in sc, 2 sc in ch-3 sp, rep from * across ending with sc in last eye, end MC — 55 (67, 79) sc.

Row 18: With A ch 2, turn. Hdc in each sc across, hdc in tch, end A.

Row 19: With MC ch 3, turn. 3 dc in first hdc, *sk 2 hdc, sc in next hdc, sk 2 hdc, 7 dc in next hdc, rep from * across ending with 4 dc in last hdc, ch 1, turn.

Row 20: Sc in first dc, *ch 2, dc7tog over (3 dc, sc, 3 dc), ch 2, sc in next dc, rep from * across ending with ch 1, turn.

Bust Shaping

Row 21: Sc in first sc, 9 dc in eye, sc in next sc, rep from * across ending with ch 3, turn.

Rows 22–24: Rep rows 12–14.

Row 25: *Sc in sc, 3 sc in ch-3 sp, sc in eye, 3 sc in ch-3 sp, rep from * across ending with sc in last sc, end MC — 73 (89, 105) sc.

Row 26: With A ch 2, turn. Hdc in each sc across, end A.

Rows 27–30: Rep rows 11–14.

Row 31: *Sc in sc, 9 dc in next eye, rep from * across ending with sc in last sc, ch 1, turn.

Back Armhole Shaping

Row 32: Sk first sc, sl st across next 4 dc, *sc in next dc, ch 3, dc9tog over (4 dc, sc, 4 dc), ch 3, rep from * across ending with sc in next dc and leaving last 5 sts unworked, ch 1, turn — 8 (10, 12) patt reps.

Row 33: Sk first sc, *3 sc in ch-3 sp, sc in eye, 3 sc in ch-3 sp, sc in sc, rep from * across to within last 2 sts, sc2tog, end MC — 63 (79, 95) sts.

Row 34: With A ch 2, turn. Hdc2tog, hdc in each sc across to within last 2 sts, hdc2tog, end A — 61 (77, 93) sts.

Row 35: With MC ch 1, turn. Sc in first hdc, sk 1 hdc, (4 hdc, 5 dc) in next hdc, *sk 3 hdc, sc in next hdc, sk 3 hdc, 9 dc in next hdc, rep from * to within last fan ending with (5 dc, 4 hdc) in next hdc, sk 1 hdc, sc in last hdc, ch 1, turn.

Row 36: Sk first sc, sl st over next 4 dc, *sc in next dc, ch 3, dc9tog over (4 dc, sc, 4 dc), ch 3, rep from * across ending with sc in next dc and leaving last 5 sts unworked, ch 1, turn — 7 (9, 11) patt reps.

Row 37: *Sc in sc, 9 dc in next eye, rep from * across ending with sc in last sc, ch 1, turn.

Row 38: Rep row 36 — 6 (8, 10) patt reps.

Row 39: *Sc in sc, 9 dc in next eye, rep from * across ending with sc in last sc, ch 3, turn.

Small–Medium Only

Row 40: Dc4tog over 4 dc, *ch 3, sc in next dc, ch 3, dc9tog over (4 dc, sc, 4 dc), rep from * across ending with dc5tog over (4 dc, sc), ch 1, turn.

Row 41: *Sc in eye, 3 sc in ch-3 sp, sc in sc, 3 sc in ch-3 sp, rep from * across ending with sc in last eye, end MC — 49 sc.

Row 42: With A ch 2, turn. Hdc in each st across, end A.

Row 43: With MC ch 3, turn. 4 dc in first hdc, *sk 3 hdc, sc in next hdc, sk 3 hdc, 9 dc in next hdc, rep from * across ending with sc in hdc, sk 3 hdc, 5 dc in tch, ch 1, turn.

Row 44: Sc in first dc, *ch 3, dc9tog over (4 dc, sc, 4 dc), ch 3, sc in next dc, rep from * across ending with sc in tch, ch 1, turn.

Continue with rows 45 and 46.

Large–1x and 2x–3x Only

Row 40: Rep row 32 — (7, 9) patt reps.

Row 41: Rep row 33 — (57, 73) sc.

Row 42: Rep row 34 — (54, 71) hdc.

Rows 43–44: Rep rows 35 and 36 — (6, 8) patt reps

Continue with rows 45 and 46.

2x–3x Only

Row 45: Rep row 37.

Row 46: Rep row 38 — (7) patt reps.

Shoulder Shaping (All Sizes)

Row 45 (45, 47): Sc in sc, 3 sc in ch-3 sp, sc in eye, 3 sc in ch-3 sp, (sc in sc, sk ch-3 sp, 9 dc in next eye, sk ch-3 sp) 4 (4, 5) times, sc in sc, 3 sc in ch-3 sp, sc in eye, sc in last sc, ch 1, turn.

Row 46 (46, 48): Sk sc, sl st over next 3 sc, sc in each of next 4 sc, dc5tog over (sc, 4 dc), sc in next dc, [(ch 3, dc9tog over (4 dc, sc, 4 dc)] 3 (3, 4) times, ch 3, dc5tog over (4 dc, sc), sc in each of next 4 sc, sl st to end.

Front Left

With MC ch 52 (62, 72).

Work rows 1–30 same as for back. St counts and patt reps are as follows.

Row 1: 5 (6, 7) patt reps.

Row 9: 41 (49, 57) sc.

Row 17: 31 (37, 43) sc.

Row 25: 41 (49, 57) sc.

Armhole Shaping

Row 31: *Sc in sc, 9 dc in next eye, rep from * across ending with sc in last sc, ch 3, turn.

Row 32: Dc4tog over 4 dc, *ch 3, sc in next dc, ch 3, dc9tog over (4 dc, sc, 4 dc), rep from * across ending with sc in next dc and leaving last 5 sts unworked, ch 1, turn — 4½ (5½, 6½) patt reps.

Row 33: Sk first sc, *3 sc in ch-3 sp, sc in eye, 3 sc in ch-3 sp, sc in sc, rep from * across ending with sc in last eye, end MC — 36 (44, 52) sts.

Row 34: With A ch 2, turn. Hdc in each sc across to within last 2 sts, hdc2tog, end A — 61 (77, 93) sts.

Row 35: With MC ch 2, turn. Sc in first hdc, sk 3 hdc, (4 hdc, 5 dc) in next hdc, *sk 3 hdc, sc in next hdc, sk 3 hdc, 9 dc in next hdc, rep from * across ending with 5 dc in last hdc, ch 1, turn.

Row 36: Sc in sc, *ch 3, dc9tog over (4 dc, sc, 4 dc), ch 3, sc in next dc, rep from * across ending with sc in next dc and leaving last 5 sts unworked, ch 1, turn — 4 (5, 6) patt reps.

Row 37: *Sc in sc, 9 dc in next eye, rep from * across ending with sc in last sc, ch 3, turn.

Row 38: Dc4tog over 4 dc, *ch 3, sc in next dc, ch 3, dc9tog over (4 dc, sc, 4 dc), rep from * across ending with sc in next dc and leaving last 5 sts unworked, ch 1, turn.

Row 39: *Sc in sc, 9 dc in next eye, rep from * across ending with 5 dc in last eye, ch 1, turn.

Small–Medium Only

Row 40: Sc in first sc, *ch 3, dc9tog over (4 dc, sc, 4 dc), ch 3, sc in next dc, rep from * across ending with ch 3, dc5tog over 5 dc, ch 1, turn.

Row 41: *Sc in eye, 3 sc in ch-3 sp, sc in sc, 3 sc in ch-3 sp, rep from * across to last eye, leave rem ch-3 and sc unworked, end MC.

Row 42: With A ch 2, turn. Hdc in each sc across, end A.

Small–Medium Neckline Shaping

Row 43: With MC ch 3, turn. 5 dc in first hdc, (sk 3 hdc, sc in next hdc, sk 3 hdc, dc9tog in next hdc) 2 times, sk 3

73

hdc, sc in next hdc, leave 7 hdc unworked, ch 1, turn — 2½ patt reps.

Row 44: Sk sc, sl st in next 4 dc, [sc in next dc, ch 3, dc9tog over (4 dc, sc, 4 dc)] 2 times, ch 3, sc in last sc, ch 1, turn. Continue with shoulder shaping.

Large–1x and 1x–2x Only

Row 40: Sc in first sc, *ch 3, dc9tog over (4 dc, sc, 4 dc), ch 3, sc in next dc, rep from * across ending with sc in next dc and leaving last 5 sts unworked, ch 1, turn. (4, 5) patt reps.

Row 41: Rep row 33 — (32, 40) sc.

Row 42: Rep row 34 — (31, 39) hdc.

Row 43: Sc in first hdc, sk 3 hdc, (4 hdc, 5 dc) in next hdc, (sk 3 hdc, sc in next hdc, sk 3 hdc, dc9tog in next hdc) 2 times, sk 3 hdc, sc in next hdc, leave 7 hdc unworked, ch 1, turn — (3, 4) patt reps.

Large–1x and 1x–2x Neckline Shaping

Row 44: Sk first sc, sl st over next 4 dc, *sc in next dc, ch 3, dc9tog over (4 dc, sc, 4 dc), ch 3, sc in next dc, rep from * across ending with sc in next dc and leaving last 5 sts unworked, ch 1, turn — (2, 3) patt reps. Continue with shoulder shaping for Large–1x only.

2x–3x Neckline Shaping

Row 45: (Sc in sc, 9 dc in next eye) 3 times, sc in sc, leaving last 5 sts unworked, ch 1, turn.

Row 46: Sk first sc, sl st over next 4 dc, [sc in next dc, ch 3, 9dctog over (4 dc, sc, 4 dc), ch 3] 2 times, sc in next dc leaving last 5 sts unworked, ch 1, turn — 2 patt reps. Continue with shoulder shaping.

Shoulder Shaping (All Sizes)

Row 45 (45, 47): Sc in sc, 3 sc in ch-3 sp, sc in eye, 3 sc in ch-3 sp, sc in sc, sk ch-3, 9 dc in next eye, sk ch-3, sc in sc, ch 1, turn — 19 sts.

Row 46 (46, 48): Sk sc, sl st over next 4 dc, sc in next dc, ch 3, dc5tog over (4 dc, sc), hdc in next sc, sc in each of next 2 sc, sl st in next sc, end — 9 sts.

Right Front

With MC ch 62 (72, 82).
Work rows 1–30 same as for back. St counts and patt reps are as follows.

Row 1: 6 (7, 8) patt reps.

Row 9: 49 (57, 65) sc.

Row 17: 37 (43, 49) sc.

Row 25: 49 (57, 65) sc.

Armhole Shaping

Row 31: *Sc in sc, 9 dc in next eye, rep from * across ending with sc in last sc, ch 1, turn.

Row 32: Sk first sc, sl st over next 4 dc, *sc in next dc, ch 3, dc9tog over (4 dc, sc, 4 dc), ch 3, rep from * across ending with sc in next dc, ch 3, 5 dcs over last 5 sts, ch 1, turn — 5½ (6½, 7½) patt reps.

Row 33: *Sc in eye, 3 sc in ch-3 sp, sc in sc, 3 sc in ch-3 sp, rep from * across ending to within 2 sts, sc2tog, end

MC — 44 (52, 60) sc.

Row 34: With A ch 2, turn. Hdc2tog, hdc in each st across, end A — 43 (53, 61) hdc.

Row 35: With MC ch 2, turn. 4 dc in first hdc, *sk 3 hdc, sc in next hdc, sk 3 hdc, 9 dc in next hdc, rep from * across ending with sc in last hdc, ch 1 turn.

Row 36: Sk first sc, sl st over next 4 dc, *sc in next dc, ch 3, dc9tog over (4 dc, sc, 4 dc), ch 3, rep from * across ending with sc in next dc, ch 3, 5 dcs over last 5 sts, ch 1, turn — 5 (6, 7) patt rep.

Row 37: *Sc in sc, 9 dc in next eye, rep from * across ending with sc in last sc, ch 1, turn.

Row 38: Sk first sc, sl st over next 4 dc, *sc in next dc, ch 3, dc9tog over (4 dc, sc, 4 dc), ch 3, rep from * across ending with sc in next dc, ch 3, dc5tog over last 5 sts, ch 3, turn — 4½ (5½, 6½) patt reps.

Small–Medium Only

Row 39: 4 dc in eye, *sc in sc, 9 dc in eye, rep from * ending with sc in sc, ch 3, turn.

Row 40: Sk sc, dc4tog over 4 dc, *ch 3, sc in next dc, ch 3, dc9tog over (4 dc, sc, 4 dc), rep from * ending with sc in tch, ch 1, turn. Continue with shoulder and neckline shaping.

Large–1x and 2x–3x Only

Row 39: 4 dc in eye, *sc in sc, 9 dc in eye, rep from * ending with sc in sc, ch 1, turn.

Row 40: Sk first sc, sl st over next 4 dc, *ch 3, sc in next dc, ch 3, dc9tog over (4 dc, sc, 4 dc), rep from * ending with sc in tch, ch 1, turn. Continue with shoulder and neckline shaping — (5, 6) patt reps.

Shoulder and Neckline Shaping

Row 41: *Sc in sc, 3 sc in ch-3 sp, sc in eye, 3 sc in ch-3 sp, rep from * across ending with sc in sc, end MC — 37 (41, 49) sc.

Row 42: With A ch 2, turn. Hdc in each st across, end A.

Row 43: Count 21 (21, 29) hdc from armhole edge and tie on MC in this st. (Sk 3 hdc, 9 dc in next hdc, sk 3 hdc, sc in next hdc) 2 (2, 3) times, sk 3 hdc, 5 hdc in last st, ch 1, turn — 2½ (2½, 3½) patt reps.

Row 44: Sc in first dc, [ch 3, dc9tog over (4 dc, sc, 4 dc), ch 3, sc in dc] 2 (2, 3) times, ch 1, turn — 2 (2, 3) patt reps. Continue with shoulder shaping for Small–Medium and Large–1x.

2x–3x Only

Row 45: (Sc in sc, sk ch-3 sp, 9 dc in eye, sk ch-3 sp) 3 times, sc in sc, ch 1, turn.

Row 46: Sk first sc, sl st in next 4 dc, [sc in next dc, ch 3, dc9tog over (4 dc, sc, 4 dc), ch 3] 2 times, sc in next dc, ch 1, turn — 2 patt reps. Continue with shoulder shaping.

Shoulder Shaping (All Sizes)

Row 45 (45, 47): Sc in sc, 9 dc in next eye, sc in next sc, 3 sc in ch-3 sp, sc in eye, sc in ch-3 sp, sc in last sc, ch 1, turn.

Row 46 (46, 48): Sk sc, sl st over next 4 sc, sc in each of next

2 sc, hdc in next sc, dc5tog over (sc, 4 dc), ch 3, sc in next dc, end.

Sleeve (Make 2)
With MC ch 44 (44, 50).

Row 1: Sc in 2nd ch from hook, *sk 2 ch, 7 dc in next ch, sk 2 ch, sc in next ch, rep from * across, ch 3, turn — 7 (7, 8) patt reps.

Row 2: Sk sc, dc3tog over next 3 dcs, *ch 2, sc in next dc, ch 2, dc7tog over (3 dc, sc, 3 dc), rep from * across ending with dc4tog over (3 dc, sc), ch 3, turn.

Row 3: 3 dc in eye, *sc in next sc, 7 dc in next eye, rep from * across ending with 4 dc in last eye, ch 1, turn.

Row 4: Sc in first sc, *ch 2, dc7tog over (3 dc, sc, 3 dc), ch 2, sc in sc, rep from * across ending with sc in tch, ch 1, turn.

Row 5: Sc in first sc, *7 dc in next eye, sc in next sc, rep from * across, ch 3, turn.

Row 6: Dc4tog over (sc, 3 dc), *ch 2, sc in next dc, ch 2, dc7tog over (3 dc, sc, 3 dc), rep from * ending with dc4tog over (3 dc, sc), ch 1, turn.

Row 7: *Sc in eye, 2 sc in ch-2 sp, sc in sc, 2 sc in ch-2 sp, rep from * across ending with sc in eye, end MC — 43 (43, 49) sc.

Row 8: With A ch 2, turn. Hdc in each sc across, end A.

Row 9: With MC ch 3, turn. 3 dc in first hdc, *sk 2 hdc, sc in next hdc, sk 2 hdc, 7 dc in next hdc, rep from * across ending with sk 2 hdc, 4 dc in tch, ch 1, turn.

Row 10: Sc in first sc, *ch 2, dc7tog over (3 dc, sc, 3 dc), ch 2, sc in sc, rep from * across ending with sc in third ch, ch 1, turn.

Row 11: Sc in first sc, *9 dc in next eye, sc in next sc, rep from * across, ch 3, turn.

Row 12: Dc4tog over 4 dc, *ch 3, sc in next dc, ch 3, dc9tog over (4 dc, sc, 4 dc), rep from * ending with dc5tog over (4 dc, sc), ch 3, turn.

Row 13: 4 dc in eye, *sc in next sc, 9 dc in next eye, rep from * across ending with 5 dc in last eye, ch 1, turn.

Row 14: Sc in first dc, ch 3, dc9tog over (4 dc, sc, 4 dc), ch 3, sc in next dc, rep from * across ending with sc in third ch, ch 1, turn.

Row 15: *Sc in sc, 3 sc in ch-3 sp, sc in eye, 3 sc in ch-3 sp, rep from * across ending with sc in sc, end MC — 57 (57, 65) sc.

Row 16: With A ch 2 turn. Hdc in each sc across, end A.

Row 17: With MC ch 1, turn. Sc in first hdc, *sk 3 hdc, 9 dc in next hdc, sk 3 hdc, sc in hdc, rep from * across, ch 3, turn.

Row 18: Dc5tog over (sc, 4 dc), *ch 3, sc in next dc, ch 3, dc9tog over (4 dc, sc, 4 dc), rep from * across ending with dc5tog over (4 dc, sc), ch 3, turn.

Rows 19–20: Rep rows 13 and 14.

Row 21: Sc in first sc, *11 dc in next eye, sc in sc, rep from * across, ch 1, turn.

Cap Shaping
Row 22: Sk first sc, sl st over next 5 dc, ch 4, *sc in next dc, ch 4, dc11tog over (5 dc, sc, 5 dc), ch 4, rep from * to within last 6 sts, leave them unworked, ch 1, turn — 6 (6, 7) patt reps.

Row 23: Sk first sc, 4 sc in ch-4 sp, sc in eye, 4 sc in ch-4 sp,

rep from * across to with last 2 sts, sc2tog, end MC — 59 (59, 69) sts.

Row 24: With A ch 2, turn. Sk first sc, hdc in each sc across to within last 2 hdc, hdc2tog, end A — 57 (57, 67) sts.

Row 25: With MC ch 1, turn. Sc in first hdc, sk 2 hdc, 11 dc in next hdc, sk 4 hdc, sc in next hdc, *sk 4 hdc, 11 dc in next hdc, sk 4 hdc, sc in next hdc, rep from * across after completing last diamond, sk 2 hdc, sc in last hdc, ch 1, turn.

Row 26: Rep row 22 — 5 (5, 6) patt reps.

Row 27: Sc in first sc, *11 dc in next eye, sc in next sc, rep from * across, ch 1, turn.

Row 28: Rep row 22 — 4 (4, 5) patt reps.

Row 29: Sc in first sc, *9 dc in next eye, sc in next sc, rep from * across, ch 1, turn.

Row 30: Rep row 22 — 3 (3, 4) patt reps. End Small-Medium.

Large–1x and 2x–3x Only
Row 31: Rep row 29.

Row 32: Rep row 22 — (2, 3) patt reps. End Large–1x.

2x–3x Only
Row 33: Rep row 29.

Row 34: Rep row 22 — (2) patt reps. End 2x–3x.

Rosette
With MC ch 40.

Row 1: 25 hdc, 2 hdc in each of next 5 ch, 2 dc in each of next 5 ch, 2 tr in each of next 5 ch, ch 3, turn.

Row 2: Sk first tr, 2 tr in each of next 25 sts, dc in each of next 10 sts, ch 4, turn.

Row 3: Sk first st, tr in next 17 sts, end.

This strip will naturally curl. You can play with different ways of forming a flower using the skinny part of the strip as the center. Keep a three-dimensional effect by letting the center sit on top. Once you have a flower you like, tack it from the back. When done with all other finishing, tack it to the collar (refer to photos).

finishing
Sew side seams from RS with mattress stitch. Sew shoulder seams from inside with sc, picking up one strand from each side of garment.

Pin the center of the sleeve cap to the shoulder seam of the garment, then continue pinning at several points to the underarm, matching up the topmost A stripe on sleeve with 2nd to top A stripe on garment. Sew this seam from RS with overhand stitch. There will be a little extra fabric (1–2") in this sleeve to ease in above the stripe. Work in ease as you sew. Sew the seam of the sleeve itself with stitch of your choice, after sewing sleeve to armhole.

Border and Collar
With RS facing, tie on MC at bottom right corner of front piece, ch 1. Work sc edging along right front from bottom up to neck, placing last st before last row where color change occurs, end off. In order to create a seamless edging with top of row, turn, tie

on A in same st, ch 2, remove hook from st, insert hook under top lps of adjacent st on color change row, pull dropped loop through. Working around corner, work 2 hdc in first sc of edging, continue working hdc in each sc to bottom, cut A and secure last st on safety pin.

With RS facing, tie on MC at top corner of left front piece just under color change, ch 1. Work sc edging down this side as on opposite side to bottom, end MC. Starting with A in top of last st, ch 2, turn. Work hdc in each sc, 2 hdc around corner, sl st to top of color change row, end.

Pick up secured loop at bottom right, change to MC by pulling MC through loop, ch 4, tr in same st, 2 tr in each hdc to first corner st. Ch 4, turn work 90 degrees and work 3 tr over post of last tr. Continuing around neckline, work 2 tr into each hdc. Continue working around neckline maintaining density of tr stitches so they ruffle slightly, place last tr before color change at top of left front piece, ch 4, turn. Continuing collar, tr into each tr, tr in ch 4 at beginning of previous row. Ch 4, turn, tr across, end.

Try on sweater and sew snap at top corner of collar.

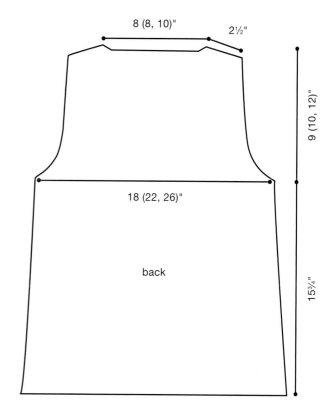

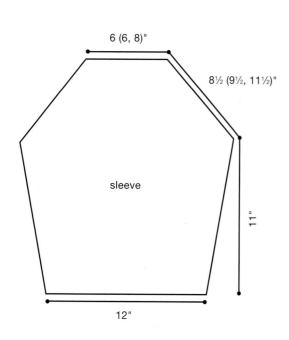

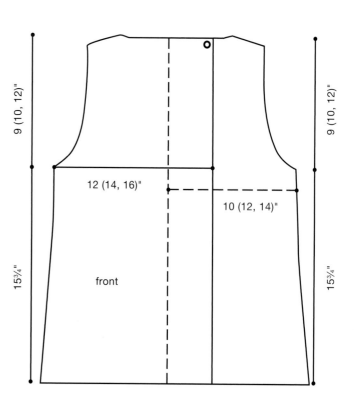

DIAMOND HEADS

In general, the easiest way to make a crocheted hat is to start at the top and work in the round. For this design, however, I wanted to try working from the bottom up, starting with the most visible part, the band, which could be wide with colorful diamonds. Then, to keep the diamond pattern going while shaping the upper portion of the hat, I gradually decreased the number of stitches in the diamond patterns. Using the same technique as in A Rose is a Rose Jacket on page 70. At the top of this hat, I had another option not available in top-down hats — leaving an opening to be gathered. This lends softness and also dimension, which in turn suggests richness to me, as if no skimping on fabric was necessary.

It was fun using "yarn ends" from a batch of stunning Berroco yarns in my stash. These patterns are meant for stash busting, so gather your most luscious leftovers, with colors that blend smoothly or contrast dramatically.

One hat is worked with two skeins of a heavy worsted tweedy yarn, Berroco's Keltic in sumptuous autumnal colors. The last crocheted hat I made looked cute, but one night last winter while I waited at a bus stop, it proved totally useless against a frigid New York wind. So for this one I went for a tight gauge and a good snug fabric. The wide band is added after completing the hat and made in a looser gauge to give it more amplitude.

Hat two is where you can choose a very special novelty yarn, like Berroco Trilogy, and feature it prominently in the hat's brim. No fun fur, though, please! The other yarns are worsted alpacas and merinos, both very soft and silky. Worked with the same size hook as the first hat, they make a closer-fitting, more svelte hat.

Remember that there's a right and wrong side of the fabric: when working in the round, one side shows all fronts of stitches, the other their backs. Generally fronts are preferable (though not always). Since the brim is folded over, you must change direction when you work it, to get the front-facing stitches showing on the opposite side.

Color work is heavy with ends to weave in, but working in the round means they can be carried on the inside, though it leaves visible strands. Personally, I think it's fine as long as you don't wear hair jewelry.

DIAMOND
HEADS pink

skill level: intermediate

finished size

One size fits most teenage or adult females

materials

Berroco Keltic (1.75 ounces/103 yards, 50 grams/95
   meters per ball) 1 ball each of:
   #5857 Teal/Wine (A)
   #5864 Pink/Wine (B)
Size H-8 (5 mm) crochet hook or size needed to obtain
   gauge
Size I-9 (5.5 mm) crochet hook for brim

gauge

1 patt rep = 3", 4 rows = 2½"

stitching technique

Each diamond has an "eye" in the center. The eye is
the last half of the dcXtog stitch, which holds all of the
double crochets together. Work X dcs into the eye on
the next row to complete the diamond pattern.

diamond stitch pattern in the round

Multiple of 8

Work designated number of foundation chains, sl st to first chain to form ring.

Rnd 1: Sc in first st (same st as sl st), *sk 3 ch, 9 dc in next st, sk 3 ch; rep from * around ending with sl st in beg sc.

Rnd 2: Ch 3 (counts as 1st dc), dc4tog over next 4 dc, ch 3, *sc in next dc, ch 3, dc9tog over (4 dc, sc, 4 dc), ch 3; rep from * around, ending with sc in next dc, ch 3, dc4tog without finishing last lp (5 lps on hook), insert hook into top of starting dc4tog, pull lp through this st and lps on hook.

Rnd 3: Ch 3 (counts as 1st dc), 3 dc into eye, *sk ch 3, sc in sc, sk ch 3, 9 dc into eye, rep from * around ending with sk ch 3, sc in sc, sk ch 3, 4 dc into last eye, sl st to top of beg ch 3.

Rnd 4: Ch 1, sc in top of ch 3, *ch 3, dc9tog over (3 dc, sc, 3 dc), ch 3, sc in next dc, rep from * ending with ch 3, dc9tog, ch 3, sl st in beg sc, turn.

Rnd 5: Ch 1, sc into first sc, *sk ch 3, 9 dc into eye, sk ch 3, sc into next sc, rep from * around ending with sk ch 3, 9 dc into eye, sk ch 3, sl st in beg sc, turn.

Rep rnds 2–5 for pattern.

changing color

To change color, pull the new yarn through the last loop of the stitch before the color change.

The unused color can be carried along the inside of hat; strands will be about 2" long. If you prefer, you may cut old yarn and tie on new yarn at every color change. That's the best choice for those who wear hair barettes or clips which may catch on the strands.

instructions

With A, ch 56, sl st to form ring.

Rnd 1: Work rnd 1 of Diamond Pattern, change color to B — 7 patt reps.

Rnd 2: Work rnd 2 of Diamond Pattern, change to A.

Rnd 3: Work rnd 3 of Diamond Pattern, change B.

Rnd 4: Work rnd 4 of Diamond Pattern.

Rnd 5: Ch 1, work rnd 5 of Diamond Pattern patt st, change to A.

Rnd 6: Work rnd 2 but do not change color at end of rnd.

Rnd 7: Ch 3, 3 dc in same st, *sk 3 ch, sc in sc, sk 3 ch, 7 dc in next eye, rep from * around ending sk 3 ch, sc in sc, sk ch 3, 3 dc in same st as starting ch 3, sl st to top of ch 3, change to B.

Rnd 8: Ch 1, sc in top of ch 3, *ch 2, dc7tog over (3 dc, sc, 3 dc) ch 2, sc in next dc, rep from * around ending with ch 2, dc7tog over (3 dc, sc, 3 dc), sl st to beg sc.

Rnd 9: Ch 1, sc in sc, *sk ch 2, 5 dc in eye, sk ch 2, sc in sc, rep from * around, ending with sl st to beg sc, change to A.

Rnd 10: Ch 3, dc2tog over next 2 dc, *ch 1, sc in next dc, ch 1, dc5tog over (2 dc, sc, 2 dc), rep from * around ending with ch 1, sc in next dc, ch 1, dc2tog without finishing last loop (3 lps on hook), insert hook in dc2tog at start of row, pull loop through this st and lps on hook.

Rnd 11: Ch 3, dc in eye, *sk ch 1, sc in sc, sk ch 1, 2 dc in next eye, rep from * around ending with sk ch 1, sc in sc, ch 1, sl st in tch. End off leaving 6" long tail.

Place tapestry needle on tail and weave in and out of the tops of stitches of last rnd, pull top of hat closed. Sew in this tail very securely.

brim

Change to larger hook.

With A, tie on at base of foundation chain at any sc, ch 1.

Rnd 1: Sc in sc, work rnd 1 of Diamond Pattern, change to B.

Rnds 2–4: Cont in Diamond Pattern, changing from B to A at end of rnd 3, end off.

DIAMOND
HEADS blue

skill level: intermediate

finished size

One size fits most teenage or adult females

materials

Berocco Pure Merino — A (1.75 ounces/92 yards,
50 grams/84 meters per ball):
Taupe (A) — approximately 40 yards
Berocco Trilogy — (1.75 ounces/80 yards, 50 grams/73
meters per ball:
Multi-color (B) — approximately 40 yards
Berocco Ultra Alpaca (3.50 ounces/215 yards, 100
grams/196 meters per ball): approximately 40
yards — Light Olive Green (C), Medium Teal (D),
Dark Teal (E)
Size H-8 (5 mm) crochet hook or size necessary to
obtain gauge
Size I-9 (5.5 mm) crochet hook for brim

gauge

1 patt rep = 2½", 4 rows = 2½"

stitching technique

Each diamond has an "eye" in the center. The eye is the
last half of the dcXtog stitch, which holds all of the double
crochets together. Work X dcs into the eye on the next row
to complete the diamond pattern.

diamond stitch pattern in the round

Multiple of 8

Work designated number of foundation chains, sl st to first chain to form ring.

Row 1: Sc in first st (same st as sl st), *sk 3 ch, 9 dc in next st, sk 3 ch; rep from * around ending with sl st in beg sc.

Row 2: Ch 3 (count as 1st dc), dc4tog over next 4 dc, ch 3, *sc in next dc, ch 3, dc9tog over (4 dc, sc, 4 dc), ch 3; rep from * around, ending with sc in next dc, ch 3, dc4tog without finishing last loop (5 lps on hook), insert hook into top of starting dc4tog, pull loop through this st and lps on hook.

Row 3: Ch 3 (count as 1st dc), 3 dc into eye, *sk ch 3, sc in sc, sk ch 3, 9 dc into eye, rep from * around ending with sk ch 3, sc in sc, sk ch 3, 4 dc into last eye, sl st to top of beg ch 3.

Row 4: Ch 1, sc in top of ch 3, *ch 3, dc9tog over (3 dc, sc, 3 dc), ch 3, sc in next dc, rep from * ending with ch 3, dc9tog, ch 3, sl st in beg sc, turn.

Row 5: Ch 1, sc into first sc, *sk ch 3, 9 dc into eye, sk ch 3, sc into next sc, rep from * around ending with sk ch 3, 9 dc into eye, sk ch 3, sl st in beg sc, turn.

Rep rows 2–5 for pattern.

Refer to stitch diagram on page 67. The st patt used is the same, but as it is worked in the round, 1 stitch at end of each row is eliminated.

instructions

Note: The first 6 rounds will be folded over to make the brim. In order to have the RS of the work facing in both the brim and the main body of the hat, you will change direction of work in row 7. With A and hook I, ch 64.

Rnd 1: Work rnd 1 of Diamond Pattern, change color to B — 8 patt reps.

Rnd 2: Work rnd 2 of Diamond Pattern.

Rnd 3: Work rnd 3 of Diamond Pattern, change color to C.

Rnd 4: Work rnd 4 of Diamond Pattern.

Rnd 5: Ch 1, work rnd 1 of Diamond Pattern, change to A.

Rnd 6: Rep rnd 2 but do not change color at end of rnd.

Rnd 7: Turn work to change direction, so that RS of brim will be showing. Work rnd 3 of Diamond Pattern, change to D.

Rnds 8 & 9: Switch to hook H and rep rnds 4 and 5, change to E.

Rnds 10 & 11: Rep rnds 2 & 3, change to D.

Rnd 12: Rep rnd 4.

Rnd 13: Ch 3, 3 dc in same st, *sk ch 3, sc in sc, sk ch 3, 7 dc in next eye, rep from * around ending with sk ch 3, sc in sc, sk ch 3, 3 dc in same st as starting ch 3, sl st to top of ch 3, change to B.

Rnd 14: Ch 1, sc in top of ch 3, *ch 2, dc7tog over (3 dc, sc, 3 dc) ch 2, sc in next dc, rep from * around ending with ch 2, dc7tog over (3 dc, sc, 3 dc), sl st in beg sc.

Rnd 15: Ch 1, sc in sc, *sk ch 2, 5 dc in eye, sk ch 2, sc in sc, rep from * around, ending with sk ch 2, dc5tog over (2 dc, sc, 2 dc) sl st in beg sc, change to A.

Rnd 16: Ch 3, dc2tog over next 2 dc, *ch 1, sc in next dc, ch 1, dc5tog over (2 dc, sc, 2 dc), rep from *around ending with ch 1, sc in dc, ch 1, dc2tog without finishing last loop (3 lps on hook), insert hook in dc2tog at start of row, pull lp through this st and lps on hook.

Rnd 17: Ch 3, dc in eye, *sk ch, 1 sc in sc, sk ch 1, 2 dc in next eye, rep from * around ending with sl st to top of beg ch 3. End off leaving 6" long tail.

Place tapestry needle on tail and weave in and out tops of stitches of last rnd, pull top of hat closed. Sew in this tail very securely.

PRECIOSILLA PURSE

The concept for this purse began with an urge to work the diamonds on the bias, that is, with rows of diamonds on a slant. To work out the concept, I printed out a copy of a finished piece of work using diamonds, then drew lines on it to see how the stitch pattern could be turned on the diagonal. It soon became clear that it was simply a matter of going from one pattern at the corner edge, to two in the next row, three in the next, etc. To actually stitch this, however, I realized it would be far easier to start at the longest edge and do decreases in the number of diamonds. Otherwise, if I started with one diamond, I'd have to keep adding chains on both sides to accommodate the added patterns, a cumbersome and inelegant procedure. Decreasing a half pattern on each row, on the other hand, is simple. It does, however, require the piece be worked in two halves.

Browsing through a marvelous book of museum-quality purses called *Bags*, published by Pepin Press, I was impressed with the fine finishing details that lift a bag into the masterpiece category — trims, tassles, special closures and handles, all of which are design opportunities. In the end, a triangular construction seemed to provide that extra touch for this design. To use part of the square as a triangular flap, the front piece had to have a straight edge at the top. Let me share the fact that I have limited gifts for visualizing structure, so these insights come to me only after many hours of staring at drawings and turning them this way and that. To top off this design, I used a crab-stitch, or reverse single crochet trim along the flap and a fancy rhinestone button for closure.

How did I come up with the peculiar name for this purse? In my other life I am a concert singer, and this is the title of a song I have performed many times. American composer Virgil Thomson created it with a text (and thus this title) by the great coiner of words, Gertrude Stein. I just love the word because it connotes something small and precious, and that's what I had in mind when making this little silk bag.

PRECIOSILLA PURSE

skill level: intermediate

finished measurement

5" x 8" (Triangle) with 12" long handle

materials

Schulana Seta-bella (1.75 ounces/137 yards, 50
   grams/125 meters per ball):
   #31 Turquoise (A) — 1 ball
   #6 Fuchsia (B) — 1 ball
Size B-1 (2.25 mm) crochet hook or size needed to
   obtain gauge

gauge

2 diamonds and 6 rows = approximately 3"

special stitches

Double crochet 9 sts together (Dc9tog): *Yo, insert
hook in designated st and pull up loop, yo and pull
through 2 lps, rep from *8 times (10 lps on hook), yo
and pull through all lps on hook, ch 1 to close.

Double crochet 5 sts together (Dc5tog): *Yo, insert
hook in designated st and pull up loop, yo and pull
through 2 lps, rep from *4 times (5 lps on hook), yo
and pull through all lps on hook, ch 1 to close.

Reverse Single Crochet (RSC): Working from left to
right (or right to left if you are left-handed), insert hook
in next st, draw a loop through and under the loop on
hook, yo, draw through 2 lps on hook.

stitching technique

Each diamond has an "eye" in the center. The eye is
the last half of the dcXtog stitch, which holds all of the
double crochets together. Work X dcs into the eye on
the next row to complete the diamond pattern.

(see Catherine's Diamond 9-dc variation on page 67)

instructions

Half Square (Triangle) for Back

Note: After changing colors, cut the yarn not in use.

With A, ch 42.

Row 1: Sc in 2nd ch from hook, *sk 3 ch, 9 dc in next ch, sk 3 ch, sc in next ch; rep from * across 4 more times, turn — 5 patt reps.

Row 2: Sk sc, sl st across each of next 3 dc, make 4th sl st by inserting hook in next dc and pulling B through stitch and loop on hook, ch 1 *sc in next dc, ch 3, dc9tog over next 9 dc, ch 3, rep from * 3 more times, ending with sc in next dc, ch 1, turn — 4 patt reps.

Row 3: *Sc in sc, sk 3 ch, 9 dc in eye, sk 3; rep from * across ending with sc in last sc, turn.

Row 4: Sk sc, sl st across each of next 4 dc, ch 1, *sc in next dc, ch 3, dc9tog over next 9 dc, ch 3, rep from * 2 more times, ending with sc in next dc, ch 1, turn — 3 patt reps.

Row 5: Rep row 3.

Row 6: Sk sc, sl st across each of next 4 dc, ch 1, *sc in next dc, ch 3, dc9tog over next 9 dc, ch 3, rep from * once, ending with sc in next dc, ch 1, turn — 2 patt reps.

Row 7: Rep row 3.

Row 8: Sk sc, sl st across each of next 3 dc, make 4th sl st by inserting hook in next dc and pulling A through stitch and loop on hook, ch 1, sc in next dc, ch 3, dc9tog over next 9 dc, ch 3, ending with sc in dc, ch 1, turn —1 patt rep.

Row 9: Rep row 3, end off.

Second Half Square for Back:

With WS facing (RS has flatter appearance), tie on A in base of foundation chain under first sc, ch 1, sc in same st, *9 dc in base of ch under 9 dc, sc in base of next sc, rep from * across.

Rep rows 2–9.

Note: The front piece is worked even at the top edge with decreases at the bottom edge as on back.

Front

With A, ch 26.

Row 1: Sc in second ch from hook, *sk 3 ch, 9 dc in next ch, sk 3 ch, sc in next ch, rep from * across 2 more times, turn — 3 patt reps.

Row 2: Sk sc, sl st across each of next 3 dc, make 4th sl st by inserting hook in next dc and pulling B through stitch and loop on hook, ch 1, *sc in next dc, ch 3, dc9tog over next 9 dc, ch 3, rep from * once, ending with sc in next dc, ch 3, dc5tog over 4 dcs and 1 sc, ch 3, turn.

Row 3: 4 dcs in eye, *sc in sc, sk ch-3, 9 dc in eye; rep from * once, ending with sk ch-3, sc in last sc, do not

ch 1, turn — 2½ patt reps.

Row 4: Sk sc, sl st across each of next 4 dc, make ch 1, *sc in next dc, ch 3, dc9tog over next 9 dc, ch 3, rep from * once, ending with sc in tch, ch 1, turn — 2 patt reps.

Row 5: *Sc in sc, sk ch-3, 9 dc in eye, sk ch-3, rep from * once, sc in final sc, do not ch 1, turn.

Row 6: Sk sc, sl st across each of next 4 dc, make ch 1, *sc in next dc, ch 3, dc9tog over next 9 dc, ch 3, sc in next dc, ch 3, dc5tog over 4 dcs and 1 sc, ch 3 — 1½ patt reps.

Row 7: 4 dcs in eye, sk ch 3, *sc in sc, sk ch-3, 9 dc in eye, sc in sc, do not ch 1, turn.

Row 8: Sk sc, sl st across each of next 4 dc, make ch 1, sc in next dc, ch 3, dc9tog overnext 9 dc, ch 3, sc in ch, ch 1 — 1 patt rep.

Row 9: 9 dc in eye, sc in sc, end off.

Tie on in same way as for second section of back and work in same manner over 3 patt reps.

Rows 2–9: Rep rows 2–9 of half front.

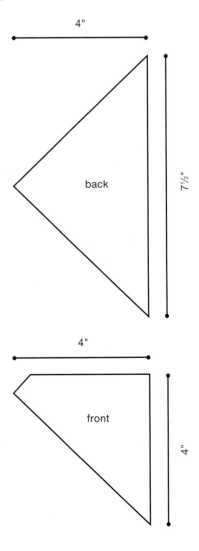

4"

7½"

back

4"

front

4"

finishing

Border and Seam

Row 1: Using larger hook and B, with WS of 2 pieces facing each other, and with RS of front facing, work sc seam beginning a top of turquoise diamond at top, around to same point opposite, change to A, turn.

Row 2: Work RSC in each sc across.

Border for Front Flap

Row 1: With RS of back facing, tie on with B at edge of row 1 of border just completed, work sc around entire flap, sl st to row 2 of border on bottom, end off.

Row 2: With RS facing, tie on A at edge of row 2 on border of bottom, work RSC around flap to center point. Place button at point where it will be sewn (see photo) and work sufficient chains to loop around button, then continue working RSC border around flap. Sl st to row 2 on border of bottom, end off.

As you weave in all ends, use them to secure any loose connection at seams.

Handle

With A, ch 56.

Row 1: Work in patt across, change to B — 7 patt reps.

Row 2: Work in patt across, secure last loop on safety pin.

Roll these 2 rows together lengthwise and close with slip stitches, picking up 1 strand from each side. Work the slip stitches close together, but loosely, to prevent pulling fabric too tight. A little curling is fine to shape the handle. Continue to work slip stitches around upper end of tube.

Now make an attachment ring as follows: Ch 6, sl st to beg of first ch to form ring, ch 1, turn. Work 8 sc in ring, end off leaving about 12" of yarn. Wrap this excess yarn around top of attachment ring several times as shown in photo, weave in ends securely. Tie on at opposite end of handle, close up end of tube with slip stitches as on opposite end, and make another attachment ring. Thread a 15" strand of A on tapestry needle and weave through flap of purse at right-most edge where it folds over. Work this thread around attachment ring of handle, taking care that the front side of the handle (which shows more of color A) is facing and that the lps lie next to one another nicely. Rep on left side. Weave in ends securely.

chapter three RIPPLES AND WAVES

The last set of bold graphic stitch patterns covered in this volume are ripples and waves, and I know I'm not alone in adoring these stitches. Why are they used in so many designs whether for fashion, afghans, or other home décor items? My theory is that designers like these wavy lines that resemble shapes in the natural world, and they present great opportunities for color work. These stitches can be tricky, however, when it comes to shaping. Methods need to be found which allow the pattern to stay intact while adding or subtracting as needed. You'll find some new techniques I've developed for this purpose in some of the projects here.

The shapes in these stitch patterns are created in two distinctly different ways. Ripples are made by clustering stitches, thereby causing a curve in the fabric, then condensing them via decreases a few stitches later, creating a curve in the opposite direction. All ripple stitches work this way, and the ripple gets steeper the more stitches are increased and decreased at the curves. For example, compare the stitch pattern used in Ripple Resort Mini with the one in Fruitcase. The first gathers 10 stitches into 2 stitches at the center of the ripple, while the second uses only 6 in the space of 2. You can see that this results in a steeper curve in the pattern used for the mini dress.

Waves, on the other hand, obtain their shape from graduating the heights of stitches. Most wave patterns alternate the wave row with a row of single crochet stitches, which helps to frame and offset the wave. I've come up with a few variations on standard waves that were great fun to create.

As in other chapters, some of the items are simple rectangles and others are shaped. To close the book with a bang, I went wild on the computer case and combined all the stitches in the book in the Fruitcase project.

Before you start stitching these projects, I urge you to review the stitching tips in Chapter 2 (Diamonds and Wheels), as most of them are applicable to the stitches in this chapter as well.

LOOKIN' GOOD IN THE HOODIE

For some time I've tried to imagine how to give wave stitches more dimension, so that they adorn a garment in a way similar to cable stitches. I tried single crochet post stitches but was not thrilled with the effect. Then I tried wrapping the post stitch around the very upper part of the stitch, just under the two top strands, rather than its stem, and voila! — this experiment worked. These little crochet discoveries are so rewarding, aren't they? In this design, these "mini-post stitches," are used, alternating with back loop stitches, to get different levels of accentuation on the waves.

This casual garment is a simple rectangle with a V-neck at the front and a hood. Most of the designing issues arose from the hood, not an item we make often and one which presents several puzzles: how long to make it, how wide to make it, where the curve at the back of the head falls, and how to get it to fold back into a wide collar when not on the head. By studying the hoods on two garments I own, I learned one thing that's odd about hoods: they can attach to a point below the neck, but must sit on the head at an angle. Think about it — that puts a real twist on getting the height and width dimensions right! This hood also needed a long angled gusset from the bottom of the V-neck to the shoulder. When you make this part you'll see some fancy shaping work.

If you want this project to be simple, don't hesitate to skip the hood altogether. You can simply finish off the V-neck with a single crochet edging and have a very wearable addition to your wardrobe.

LOOKIN' GOOD IN THE HOODIE

skill level: intermediate

size

Small/Medium (Large)

finished measurements

Bust, 36 (44)"
Length from shoulder to hem, 24" (25½")

materials

RY Classic Cotton Jeans Yarn, 100% cotton (1.75 ounces/82
   yards, 50 grams/75 meters per ball):
   #368 Shingle — 12 (14) balls
Size G-6 (4.00 mm) crochet hook or size needed to obtain gauge

gauge

2 patt reps = 8"
6 rows in patt = 2¼"

stitching tip

Working single crochet stitches into curvy rows: Here's an
instance where some flexibility in the tension of your stitches can
be an asset. The row forming the wave is, by definition, curvy,
making the space between stitches a bit larger than in straight
rows. In addition, as crochet stitches get taller, they tend to
widen as well. Therefore, when you work a row of single crochet
stitches into a wavy row, you want to avoid making them too
tight, or they will pinch the fabric and fight your wave rather than
heighten it. So, work these single crochet rows more loosely than
you normally would by keeping those fingers and wrists supple
and observing your fabric as it comes off the hook.

special stitches

Single crochet around front mini post (FMPsc): This post stitch is worked around the smaller post just under the 2 top lps. Insert hook around mini-post and pull up loop, yo, pull loop through. Count these rows when done to make sure you have not changed the stitch count — as stitch is displaced to the right slightly, it's easy to get off count! Work last st into tch of previous row. There will be no post to work around. Work these stitches loosely, otherwise you may see them flattening out the wave pattern.

Single crochet 2 together around front mini post (FMPsc2tog): * Insert hook around mini post of next st and draw up loop, rep from * (3 lps on hook), yo, draw through all 3 lps on hook.

Single crochet 3 together around front mini post (FMPsc3tog): * Insert hook around mini post of next st and draw up loop, rep from * 2 times, (4 lps on hook), yo, draw through all 4 lps on hook.

Front loop single crochet 3 together (FLsc3tog): * Insert hook in FL of next st and draw up loop, rep from * (4 lps on hook), yo, draw through all 4 lps on hook.

Treble crochet 3 together (tr3tog): Work 3 treble crochets without finishing last lps, (4 lps on hook), yo, draw through all lps on hook.

instructions

Back
Ch 65 (79).

Row 1: Sc in 2nd ch from hook and each ch across, turn — 64 (78) sts.

Row 2: Ch 1, sc in first st, *sc in next st, 2 hdc, 2 dc**, 3 tr, 2 dc, 2 hdc, 2 sc; rep from * across, ending sc, 2 hdc, 2 dc, 2 tr, turn.

Row 3: Ch 1, FLsc in each st across, turn.

Row 4: Ch 4 (counts as first tr), *tr, 2 dc, 2 hdc, 2 sc, sc, 2 hdc, 2 dc, tr; rep from * across ending tr, 2 dc, 2 hdc, 2 sc; rep from * across, turn.

Row 5: Ch 1, FLsc in each st across, turn.

Row 6: Rep row 2.

Row 7: Ch 1, FMPsc across, ending with sc in last st, turn.

Row 8: Rep row 4.

Row 9: Rep row 7, working last st in top of tch, turn.

Rows 10–39: Rep rows 2–9 ending with row 7, turn — 64 (78) sts.

Armhole Shaping

Row 40: Ch 1, sk first st, sl st across 3 sts, ch 3 (counts as dc), 2 hdc, 2 sc, *sc, 2 hdc, 2 dc, 3 tr, 2 dc**, 2 hdc, 2 sc; rep from * across ending last rep at **, hdc, leaving last 3 sts unworked, turn — 58 (72) sts.

Row 41: Ch 1, sk first st, FMPsc in each st across, sk tch, turn — 56 (70) sts.

Row 42: Ch 3 (counts as first dc), dc in next st, 2 tr, *tr, 2 dc, 2 hdc, 3 sc, 2 hdc**, 2 dc, 2 tr; rep from * across ending last rep at **, turn.

Row 43: Ch 1, sk first st, FLsc in each st across, leave last st unworked, turn — 54 (68) sts.

Row 44: Ch 2 (counts as first hdc), 2 sc, *sc, 2 hdc, 2 dc, 3 tr**, 2 dc, 2 hdc, 2 sc; rep from * across ending last rep at **, dc, turn.

Row 45: Rep row 43, turn — 52 (66) sts.

Row 46: Ch 4 (counts as first tr), tr, *tr, 2 dc, 2 hdc, 3 sc, 2 hdc, 2 dc, 2 tr, 2 dc, 2 hdc, 2 sc; rep from * across ending with sc, turn.

Row 47: Rep row 41, turn — 50 (64) sts.

Row 48: Ch 1, sc in first st, *sc, 2 hdc, 2 dc**, 3 tr, 2 dc, 2 hdc, 2 sc; rep from * across ending last rep at **, 2 tr, turn.

Small/Medium

Row 49: Ch 1, FMPsc in each st across, sc in last st, turn.

Row 50: Ch 4 (counts as first tr), *tr, 2 dc, 2 hdc**, 3 sc, 2 hdc, 2 dc, 2 tr; rep from * across ending last rep at ** 2 sc, turn.

Row 51: Ch 1, FLsc, in each st across working last st in top of tch, turn.

Row 52: Ch 1, sc, *sc, 2 hdc, 2 dc**, 3 tr, 2 dc, 2 hdc, 2 sc; rep from * across ending last rep at **, 2 tr, turn.

Row 53: Rep row 51.

Row 54: Rep row 50.

Row 55: Rep row 49.

Row 56: Rep row 52.

Row 57: Rep row 49.

Shoulder Shaping

Row 58: Ch 1, sk first st, sl 3 sts, 3 sc, 3 hdc, 3 dc, 3 sc, 21 tr, 3 dc, 3 hdc, 3 sc, sl next st, leave rem sts unworked — 42 sts.

Large

Row 49: Ch 1, sk first st, FMPsc in each st across, sk tch, turn — 62 sts.

Row 50: Ch 4 (counts as first tr), 2 dc, 2 hdc, 2 sc, *sc, 2 hdc, 2 dc, 3 tr, 2 dc, 2 hdc**, sc; rep from * across ending, last rep at **, sc, turn.

Row 51: Ch 1, sk first st, FLsc in each st across, leave last st unworked, turn — 60 sts.

Row 52: Ch 2 (counts as first hdc), hdc, 2 dc, 2 tr, *tr, 2 dc, 2 hdc, 3 sc, 2 hdc, 2 dc**, 2 tr; rep from * across ending last rep at **, turn.

Row 53: Rep row 51 — 58 sts.

Row 54: Ch 3 (counts as first dc), 2 hdc, 2 sc, *sc, 2 hdc, 2 dc, 3 tr, 2 dc**, 2 hdc, 2 sc; rep from * across ending last rep at **, hdc, turn.

Row 55: Rep row 49 — 56 sts.

Row 56: Ch 3 (counts as first dc), dc, 2 tr, *tr, 2 dc, 2 hdc, 3 sc, 2 hdc**, 2 dc, 2 tr; rep from * across ending last rep at **, turn.

Row 57: Rep row 49 — 54 sts.

Row 58: Ch 2 (counts as first hdc), 2 sc, *sc, 2 hdc, 2 dc, 3 tr**, 2 dc, 2 hdc, 2 sc; rep from * across ending last rep at **, dc, turn.

Row 59: Ch 1, FLsc, in each st across working last st in top of tch, turn — 54 sts.

Row 60: Ch 3 (counts as first dc), 2 tr, *tr, 2 dc, 2 hdc, 3 sc**, 2 hdc, 2 dc, 2 tr; rep from * across ending last rep at **, hdc.

Row 61: Rep row 59.

Shoulder Shaping

Row 62: Ch 1, sk first st, sl 5 sts, 3 sc, 3 hdc, 3 dc, 3 sc, 21 tr, 3 dc, 3 hdc, 3 sc, sl next st, leave rem sts unworked — 42 sts.

Front

Ch 65 (79).

Rows 1–39: Work same as back.

Neckline Left Panel
Small/Medium

Row 40: Ch 1, sk first st, sl 3 sts, ch 3 (counts as dc), 2 hdc, sc, * 2 sc, 2 hdc, 2 dc, 3 tr, 2 dc**, 2 hdc, 2 sc; rep from * across ending last rep at **, turn — 29 sts.

Row 41: Ch 1, sk first st, FMPsc in each st across, sc in last st, leave tch unworked, turn — 27 sts.

Row 42: Ch 3 (counts as first dc), dc, 2 tr, *tr, 2 dc, 2 hdc, 3

sc**, 2 hdc, 2 dc, 2 tr; rep from * ending last rep at **, hdc, turn.

Row 43: Ch 1, sk first st, FLsc in each st across, sk tch, ch 2, turn — 25 sts.

Row 44: Ch 2 (counts as hdc), 2 sc, * sc, 2 hdc, 2 dc, 3 tr**, 2 dc, 2 hdc, 2 sc; rep from * across ending last rep at **.

Row 45: Rep row 43, turn — 23 sts.

Row 46: Ch 4 (counts as first tr), tr, *tr, 2 dc, 2 hdc**, 3 sc, 2 hdc, 2 dc, 2 tr; rep from * ending last rep at **, 2 sc.

Row 47: Rep row 41, turn — 21 sts.

Row 48: Ch 1, sc, *sc, 2 hdc, 2 dc, 3 tr, 2 dc**, 2 hdc, 2 sc; rep from * across ending last rep at **, tr — 20 sts.

Row 49: Ch 1, sk first st, FMPsc in each st across, turn — 20 sts.

Row 50: Ch 4 (counts as first tr), *tr, 2 dc, 2 hdc**, 3 sc, 2 hdc, 2 dc, 2 tr; rep across ending last rep at **, turn.

Row 51: Ch 1, sk first st, FLsc in each st across ending FLsc in tch — 19 sts.

Row 52: Ch 1, 2 sc, 2 hdc, 2 dc, 3 tr, 2 dc, 2 hdc, 3 sc, 2 hdc, dc.

Row 53: Rep row 51 — 18 sts.

Row 54: Ch 4 (counts as first tr), tr, 2 sc, 2 hdc, 3 sc, 2 hdc, 2 dc, 3 tr, 2 dc.

Row 55: Rep row 49 — 17 sts.

Row 56: Ch 1, 2 sc, 2 hdc, 2 dc, 3 tr, 2 sc, 2 hdc, 3 sc, hdc.

Row 57: Rep row 49 — 16 sts.

Shoulder Shaping

Row 58: Ch 1, sk first st, sl 3 sts, 3 sc, 3 hdc, 3 dc, tr, tr3tog, end off — 11 sts.

Large

Row 40: Sk first st, sl 3 sts, ch 3 (counts as first dc), dc, 2 sc, * sc, 2 hdc, 2 dc, 3 tr, 2 dc, 2 hdc, 2 sc; rep from * across ending sc, 2 hdc, dc — 36 sts.

Row 41: Ch 1, sk first st, FMPsc in each st across, sc in last st, leave tch unworked, turn — 34 sts.

Row 42: Ch 3 (counts as first dc), 3 tr, 2 dc, 2 hdc, 2 sc, *sc, 2 hdc, 2 dc, 3 tr, 2 dc**, 2 hdc, 2 sc; rep from * across ending last rep at **, turn.

Row 43: Ch 1, sk first st, FLsc in each st across, sk tch, turn — 32 sts.

Row 44: Ch 1, 2 sc, * sc, 2 hdc, 2 dc, 3 tr, 2 dc, 2 hdc, 2 sc; rep from * across ending sc, turn.

Row 45: Rep row 43, turn — 30 sts.

Row 46: Ch 4 (counts as first tr), tr, 2 dc, 2 hdc, 2 sc, *sc, 2 hdc, 2 dc, 3 tr**, 2 dc, 2 hdc, 2 sc; rep from * across ending last rep at **, turn.

Row 47: Rep row 41, turn — 28 sts.

Row 48: Ch 1, sc, *sc, 2 hdc, 2 dc, 3 tr, 2 dc, 2 hdc**, 2 sc; rep from * across ending last rep at**, sc, turn.

Row 49: Rep row 41, turn — 26 sts.

Row 50: Ch 4 (counts as first tr), 2 tr, 2 dc, 2 hdc, 2 sc, *sc, 2 hdc, 2 dc**, 3 tr, 2 dc, 2 hdc, 2 sc; rep from * across ending last rep at **, turn.

Row 51: Rep row 43 — 24 sts.

Row 52: Ch 2 (counts as first hdc), hdc, 2 dc, 3 tr, 2 dc, 2 hdc, 3 sc, 2 hdc, 2 dc, 3 tr, 2 dc, hdc.

Row 53: Rep row 43 — 22 sts.

Row 54: Ch 3 (counts as first dc), 2 hdc, 3 sc, 2 hdc, 2 dc, 3 tr, 2 dc, 2 hdc, 3 sc, 2 hdc.

Row 55: Rep row 41 — 20 sts.

Row 56: Ch 3 (counts as first dc), dc, 3 tr, 2 sc, 2 hdc, 3 sc, 2 hdc, 2 dc, 3 tr, dc.

Row 57: Rep row 41 — 18 sts.

Row 58: Ch 2 (counts as first hdc), 3 sc, 2 hdc, 2 dc, 3 tr, 2 dc, 2 hdc, 3 sc.

Row 59: Ch 1, FLsc in each st across — 18 sts.

Row 60: Ch 3 (counts as first dc), 3 tr, 2 dc, 2 hdc, 3 sc, 2 hdc, 2 dc, 3 tr.

Row 61: Rep row 59 — 18 sts.

Shoulder Shaping

Row 62: Sk first st, sl st over next 4 sts, 3 sc, 3 hdc, 3 dc, tr, tr3tog, end off — 11 sts.

Neckline Right Panel
Small/Medium

Row 40: With RS facing, tie on in first unworked st next to dividing point, ch 2 (counts as first hdc), hdc, 2 sc, *sc, 2 hdc, 2 dc, 3 tr, 2 dc**, 2 hdc, 2 sc; rep from * across ending last rep at **, hdc, turn — 29 sts.

Row 41: Ch 1, sk first st, FMPsc in each st across, leave tch unworked, turn — 27 sts.

Row 42: Ch 4 (counts as first tr, tr, *tr, 2 dc, 2 hdc**, 3 sc, 2 hdc, 2 dc, 2 tr; rep from * ending last rep at **, dc, turn.

Row 43: Ch 1, sk first st, FLsc in each st across, leave tch unworked, turn — 25 sts.

Row 44: Ch 1, 2 sc, * sc, 2 hdc, 2 dc, 3 tr**, 2 dc, 2 hdc, 2 sc; rep from * across ending last rep at **, dc, turn.

Row 45: Rep row 43, turn — 23 sts.

Row 46: Ch 4 (counts as first tr), 2 dc, 2 hdc, 3 sc, 2 hdc, 2 dc, 3 tr, 2 dc, 2 hdc, 3 sc, hdc, turn.

Row 47: Rep row 41 — 21 sts.

Row 48: Ch 1, *sc, 2 hdc, 2 dc**, 3 tr, 2 dc, 2 hdc, 2 sc; rep from * ending last rep at **, 2 tr, turn.

Row 49: Ch 1, FMPsc in each st across to last 2 st, FMPsc2tog, turn — 20 sts.

Row 50: Ch 3 (counts as first dc), dc, 2 hdc, 3 sc, 2 hdc, 2 dc, 3 tr, 2 dc, 2 hdc, 2 sc, turn.

Row 51: Ch 1, FLsc in each st across, leave tch unworked, turn — 19 sts.

Row 52: Ch 2, (counts as first hdc), 2 dc, 3 tr, 2 dc, 2 hdc, 3 sc, 2 hdc, 2 dc, 2 tr, turn.

Row 53: Rep row 51, turn — 18 sts.

Row 54: Ch 2 (counts as first hdc), hdc, 3 sc, 2 hdc, 2 dc, 3 tr, 2 dc, 2 hdc, 2 sc, turn.

Row 55: Rep row 49, turn — 17 sts.

Row 56: Ch 3 (counts as first dc), 3 tr, 2 dc, 2 hdc, 3 sc, 2 hdc, 2 dc, 2 tr.

Row 57: Ch 1, Rep row 49, turn — 16 sts.

Shoulder Shaping

Row 58: [Ch 4, tr2tog (4 counts as tr3tog)], tr, 3 dc, 3 hdc, 3 sc, sl st to next sc, end off — 11 sts.

Large

Row 40: With RS facing, tie on in first unworked st next to dividing point, ch 3 (counts as first dc), dc, 2 tr, * tr, 2 dc, 2 hdc, 3 sc, 2 hdc, 2 dc, 2 tr: rep from * across

ending tr, 2 dc, hdc — 36 sts.

Row 41: Ch 1, FMPsc in each st across, leave tch unworked, turn — 34 sts.

Row 42: Ch 2 (counts as first hdc), 2 sc, *sc, 2 hdc, 2 dc, 3 tr, 2 dc, 2 hdc, 2 sc; rep from * across ending sc, 2 hdc.

Row 43: Ch 1, sk first st, FLsc in each st across, leave tch unworked, turn — 32 sts.

Row 44: Ch 4 (counts as first tr) tr, *tr, 2 dc, 2 hdc, 3 sc, 2 hdc, 2 dc, 2 tr; rep from * across ending tr, dc, turn.

Row 45: Rep row 43 — 30 sts.

Row 46: Ch 1, sc, *sc, 2 hdc, 2 dc, 3 tr, 2 dc, 2 hdc, 2 sc; rep from * across ending with sc.

Row 47: Rep row 41 — 28 sts.

Row 48: Ch 3 (counts as first dc), dc, 2 hdc, 2 sc, *sc, 2 dc, 2 hdc, 3 tr**, 2 hdc, 2 dc, 2 sc; rep from * across ending last rep at **.

Row 49: Ch 1, FMPsc in each st across to last 2 sts, FMPsc-2tog, turn — 26 sts.

Row 50: Ch 2 (counts as first hdc), 2 dc, 3 tr, 2 dc, 2 hdc, 3 sc, 2 hdc, 2 dc, 3 tr, 2 dc, 2 hdc, 2 sc, turn.

Row 51: Rep row 43 — 24 sts.

Row 52: Ch 3 (counts as first dc), 2 hdc, 3 sc, 2 hdc, 2 dc, 3 tr, 2 dc, 2 hdc, 3 sc, 2 hdc, 2 dc, turn.

Row 53: Rep row 43 — 22 sts.

Row 54: Ch 3 (counts as first dc), dc, 3 tr, 2 dc, 2 hdc, 3 sc, 2 hdc, 2 dc, 3 tr, 2 dc, hdc, turn.

Row 55: Rep row 49 — 20 sts.

Row 56: Ch 2 (counts as first hdc), 3 sc, 2 hdc, 2 dc, 3 tr, 2 dc, 2hdc, 3 sc, 2 hdc, turn.

Row 57: Rep row 49 — 18 sts.

Row 58: Ch 4 (counts as first tr), 2 tr, 2 sc, 2 hdc, 3 sc, 2 hdc, 2 dc, 3 tr, dc, turn.

Row 59: Ch 1, FLsc in each st across.

Row 60: Ch 1, 3 sc, 2 hdc, 2 dc, 3 tr, 2 dc, 2 hdc, 3 sc, hdc, turn.

Row 61: Rep row 59.

Shoulder Shaping

Row 62: [Ch 4, tr2tog (counts as tr3tog)], tr, 3 dc, 3 hdc, 3 sc, sl st in next st, end off — 11 sts.

Hood Left Side

The hood has shaped "gussets" which attach to front V-neck. The shaping for these gussets occurs on the first 10 rows.
Ch 72 (86).

Row 1: Sc in 2nd ch from hook and each ch to end — 71 (85) sts.

Row 2: Ch 1, sc, *sc, 2 hdc, 2 dc, 3 tr, 2 dc, 2 hdc, 2 sc; rep from * across.

Row 3: Ch 1, FMPsc in each st to within last 7 sts, sl st in next st (this will be the 3rd tr in patt), leave rem st unworked, turn. 64 (78) sts.

Row 4: Ch 1, sk first st, sl st in next st, *sc, 2 hdc, 2 dc, 3 tr, 2 dc, 2 hdc, 2 sc; rep from * across ending sc, 2 hdc, 2 sc, 2 tr, turn.

Row 5: Rep row 2 — 57 (71) sts.

Row 6: Ch 1, sk first st, sl st in next st, *sc, 2 hdc, 2 dc, 3 tr, 2 dc, 2 hdc, 2 sc; rep from * across, turn.

Row 7: Ch 1, FLsc in each st to within last 7 sts, sl st in next st (this will be the 3rd tr in patt), leave rem st unworked, turn — 50 (64) sts.

Row 8: Rep row 4.

Row 9: Rep row 7 — 43 (57) sts.

Row 10: Ch 1, sc, *sc, 2 hdc, 2 dc, 3 tr, 2 dc, 2 hdc, 2 sc; rep from * across, turn.

Small/Medium Only

Row 11: Ch 1, FMPsc across, sc in last st, turn

Row 12: Ch 4 (counts as first tr), tr, 2 dc, 2 hdc, 2 sc, *sc, 2 hdc, 2 sc, 3 tr, 2 dc, 2 hdc, 2 sc; rep from * across ending sc, 2 hdc, 2 sc, 2 tr — 43 sts.

Row 13: Rep row 11.

Row 14: Rep row 10.

Large Only

Row 11: Ch 1, FMPsc in each st to within last 7 sts, sl st in next st (this will be the 3rd tr in patt), leave rem st unworked, turn.

Row 12: Ch 4 (counts as first tr), *tr, 2 dc, 2 hdc, 3 sc, 2 hdc, 2 dc, 2 tr; rep from * across ending tr, 2 dc, 2 hdc, 2 sc — 50 sts.

Row 13: Rep row 3 — 43 sts.

Row 14: Ch 1, sc, *sc, 2 hdc, 2 dc, 3 tr, 2 dc, 2 hdc, 2 sc; rep from across.

Head Shaping (All Sizes)

Row 15: Ch 1, sk first st, FLsc2tog, Flsc across rem sts, turn — 41 sts.

Row 16: Ch 4 (counts as first tr), tr, 2 dc, 2 hdc, 2 sc *sc, 2 hdc,

2 sc, 3 tr, 2 dc, 2 hdc, sc; rep from * across ending sc, hdc, hdc2tog (to produce smooth edge), turn — 39 sts.

Row 17: Ch 1, sk first st, FLsc2tog, FLsc in each st across, turn — 37 sts.

Row 18: Ch 1, sc, *sc, 2 hdc, 2 sc, 2 dc, 3 tr, 2 dc, 2 hdc, sc; rep from * across ending sc, 2 hdc, 2 dc, tr3tog, turn — 35 sts.

Row 19: Ch 1, sk first st, FMP2tog, FMP in each st across, turn — 33 sts.

Row 20: Ch 4 (counts as first tr) *tr, 2 dc, 2 hdc, 3 sc, 2 hdc, 2 dc, 2 tr; rep from * across ending tr, dc3tog (for smooth edge), turn — 31 sts.

Row 21: Ch 1, FMPsc in each st across, sc in tch, end off.

Hood Right Side

Note: To make smoothest edge possible where decrease occurs, the wave patt rows have last st worked into a sl st. This means all sc rows are 1 st short of st count for row that comes after.
Ch 72 (86).

Row 1: Sc in 2nd ch from hook and each ch to end, turn — 71 (85) sts.

Row 2: Ch 1, sc, *sc, 2 hdc, 2 dc, 3 tr, 2 dc, 2 hdc, 2 sc; rep from * across, turn.

Row 3: Sk first st, sl st over next 7 st, FMPsc in next st and in each st across ending sc in last st, turn — 63 (77) sts.

Row 4: Ch 4 (counts as first tr), *tr, 2 dc, 2 hdc, 3 sc, 2 hdc, 2 dc, 2 tr; rep from * across ending tr, 2 dc, 2 hdc, sc, sl st in next st, turn.

Row 5: Ch 1, sk first sc, sl st over next 7 st, FMPsc in each st across, sc in tch 1, turn — 56 (70) sts.

Row 6: Ch 1, sc, *sc, 2 hdc, 2 dc, 3 tr, 2 dc, 2 hdc**, 2 sc; rep from * across ending last rep at **, sc, turn.

Row 7: Ch 1, sk first sc, sl st over next 7 st, FLsc in each st across, turn — 49 (63) sts.

Row 8: Ch 4 (counts as first tr), *tr, 2 dc, 2 hdc, 3 sc, 2 sc, 2 tr; rep from * ending tr, 2 sc, 2 hdc, sc, sl st in next st, ch 1 turn.

Row 9: Ch 1, sk first sc, sl st over next 7 st, FLsc in each st across, turn — 42 (56) sts.

Row 10: Ch 1, sc, *sc, 2 hdc, 2 dc, 3 tr, 2 dc, 2 hdc, 2 sc (last sc in sl st); rep from * across, turn — 43 (57) sts.

Row 11: Ch 1, FMPsc in each st across, st in last st — 43 (56) sts.

Row 12: Ch 4, (counts as first tr), *tr, 2 dc, 2 hdc, 3 sc, 2 hdc, 2 dc, 2 tr; rep from * across, turn.

Row 13: Rep row 11.

Row 14: Rep row 10.

Head Shaping

Row 15: Ch 1, FLsc in each st across to within last 3 st, FLsc3tog, turn — 41 (54) sts.

Row 16: Ch 1, sk first st, sl st over next st, 2 hdc, 2 sc, *sc, 2 hdc, 2 dc, 3 tr, 2 dc, 2 hdc, 2 sc; rep across ending sc, 2 hdc, 2 dc, 2 tr, turn – 39 (52) sts.

Row 17: Rep row 15, turn — 37 (50) sts.

Row 18: Ch 4, tr3tog (with ch 4 counts as 1 st), 2 dc, 2 hdc, 2 sc, * sc, 2 hdc, 2 dc, 3 tr, 2 dc, 2 hdc, 2 sc; rep from * across, turn 35 (48) sts.

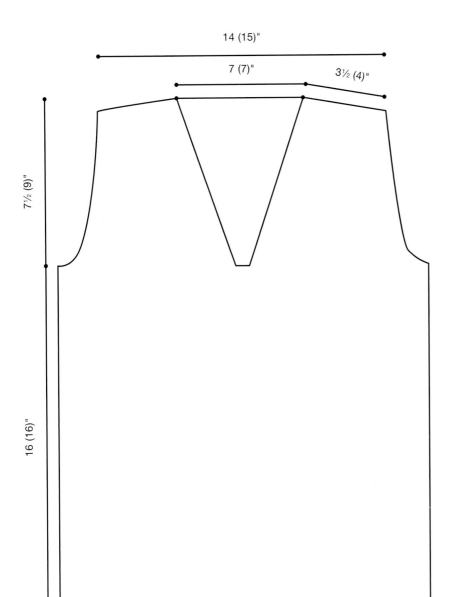

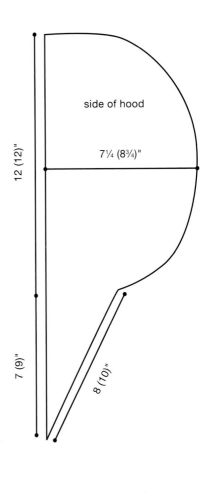

Row 19: Ch 1, FMPsc in each st to within last 3 st, FMP3tog, turn — 33 (46) sts.

Row 20: Ch 3, dc3tog (with ch 3 counts as 1 st), 2 tr, *tr, 2 dc, 2 hdc, 3 sc, 2 hdc, 2 dc, 2 tr; rep from * across, turn — 31 (44) sts.

Row 21: Ch 1, FMPsc in each st across, end off.

finishing

Sew side seams from WS using mattress stitch. Sew shoulder seams from inside using sc. You may wish to use one size smaller hook for this seam to make it easier to work into slip stitches.

Work sc edging around armholes, counting stitches and making sure the number between underarm seam and shoulder seam are the same on the front and back pieces. Model has 30 sc between each shoulder and underarm seam, but you may find this number varies depending on how tightly you work. Larger size will have 5 to 10 additional sc between shoulder and underarm seams.

Pin two halves of hood together and sew center seam from RS with mattress stitch.

Measure each side of V-neck of front — they should be the same. Measure angled edges of hood gussets. If they are not the same as V-neck, steam lightly and stretch to fit.

Beginning at gusset points, pin hood to V-neck so gusset ends at shoulder. Sew this part first, before sewing back of hood to neckline. You can use overhand stitch and hide any irregular edges under the stitches. End off at shoulder and secure well. Returning to center V-neck point, overlap one gusset edge over the other and sew down, then secure the point onto main body of garment with a few tacked stitches underneath (otherwise it will ride up when worn). Pin center of hood back to center of neckline, then pin to remainder of neckline, distributing any excess fabric in the hood fabric equally. Sew from inside with overhand stitch, easing in excess fabric as you go.

MAIDEN'S CORSET

Dazzling novelty yarns often require considerable ingenuity to get good results in crochet. The shiny or textured bits that beckon us may interfere with crisp stitch definition. Here's where I opt for one of the bold stitch patterns that creates a strong visual element where stitch definition is lacking. A particular novelty yarn, Skacel's Gentry, really appealed to me, but worked up into a rather stiff fabric. Instead of fighting that, I used it for a belt, where this quality is an asset. The layered effects and long, tunic-like sweaters now fashionable provide great opportunities for sporting a wide belt like this, and it's a quick project you can make with a small amount of yarn.

It's nice to make a belt vertically, so that you can try it on as you go and stop when it's long enough. With this in mind, I worked one wave pattern, and it seemed just the right size for a wide belt. To make the wave really stand out, it's framed with open work stitches. As this yarn has lots of character, and the belt is not meant to be shy, I added a bobble in the middle of the wave for even more pizzazz.

You'll notice that there are rows of single crochet stitches next to the wave rows. The main reason for this is to ensure that in the wave rows, the fronts of stitches are on the right side of the fabric. With a yarn of this texture, the backs of stitches can be clunky-looking, best reserved for less noticeable rows.

Belts can be closed in all sorts of ways, and finding the right buckle is like going on a treasure hunt—you know it's out there somewhere! In New York's fashion industry district, there are a few blocks lined with sewing novelty shops, mostly crammed little places with too much to choose from. I love to visit them, not only to browse, but also because many fashion industry people are shopping right along side you. More than once I've asked for, and received, expert advice about a button, buckle, or trim from a fellow customer. In a crowded aisle of one of these shops, a nice fellow who clearly knew his way around helped me find just the right buckle for this belt. The belt is designed so you can adapt the size of the added on flap to fit almost any size buckle. Nevertheless, in order to find a buckle that's a great match in style and color, I recommend having the belt, or a swatch of it, with you when you shop. Happy hunting!

MAIDEN'S CORSET

skill level: easy

size
Small/Medium (Large)

finished measurements
4" x 27" without buckle

materials

Skacel Collection Gentry (1.75 ounces/105 yards, 50 grams/96 meters per ball):
  #07 Red — 2 balls
Size F-5 (3.75 mm) hook or size needed to obtain gauge
Two-sided, wide, cinch-belt type buckle, approximately 3" in length
Note: A narrower buckle can be used. Be sure to bring a substantial swatch when you shop for the buckle!

gauge
17 sts in patt = 4"
6 rows (1 patt rep) = approximately 2½"

stitching tip
Bobbles That Pop: Sometimes you want bobbles that really pop out of the fabric. There are two ways to enhance the "pop factor:" additional stitches in the bobble, and closing the bobble tightly on your last loop. You can experiment with this, and feel free to adjust the number of double crochet stitches in your bobble, or even add some treble stitches, if you find it improves your results.

special stitch

Dc5tog (Bobble): (Yo, insert hook in designated st, yo, pull up loop, yo, pull through 2 lps) 5 times. Yo draw yarn through all 6 lps on hook, ch 1. Push bobble from WS so it pops on RS. For pleasing bobbles, make stitches tall.

instructions

Ch 18.

Row 1: Sc in 2nd ch from hook, sc in next ch, hdc in each of next 2 ch, dc in each of next 2 ch, tr in each of next 2 ch, dc5tog in next ch, tr in each of next 2 ch, dc in each of next 2 ch, hdc in each of next 2 ch, sc in each of next 2 ch, ch 1, turn — 17 sts.

Row 2: Sc in each st across, ch 4 (counts as dc and ch 1), turn.

Row 3: Sk first 2 st,* dc in next st, ch 1, sk next st, rep from * across, ending dc in last sc, ch 1, turn.

Row 4: *Sc in dc, sc in ch-1 sp, rep from * across ending sc in 3rd ch of tch, ch 4, turn.

Row 5: Tr in 2nd sc, dc in each of next 2 sc, hdc in each of next 2 sc, sc in each of next 5 sc, hdc in each of next 2 sc, dc in each of next 2 sc, tr in each of next 2 sc, ch 4, turn.

Row 6: Rep row 3, ch 1 turn.

Row 7: Sc in first dc, sc in ch-1 sp, hdc in next dc, hdc in ch-1 sp, dc in next dc, dc in ch-1 sp, tr in next dc, tr in ch-1 sp, dc5tog in next dc, tr in next ch-1 sp, tr in next dc, dc in ch-1 sp, dc in next dc, hdc in ch-1 sp, hdc in dc, sc in next ch-1 sp (this is the 4th ch of tch), sc in 3rd ch of tch, ch 1, turn.

Rep rows 2–7 until belt is desired length.

Determine the length by trying it on around waist as you work. Measure the width of both sides of your belt buckle and be sure to substract this from the finished length of your belt. End with row 2 of pattern, so that belt has bobbles at both ends.

finishing

With RS facing, work sc edging along long edges of belt, working 1 sc in sc stitches, 2 sc in dc stitches, 3 sc in tr stitiches. Work 2 sc around all ch 2 sp. End off and rep on opposite edge.

Buckle Flap

We will work a flap consisting of 2 rows of dc to wrap around the bar of the buckle. Center buckle along belt edge and determine how many stitches are needed to cover the bar. Make sure you make the same number of stitches at either side of the center stitch, which has a bobble in it. Model has 13 dc, therefore I counted 6 st to the right of center and tied on. Ch 3, dc in each of next 12 st, ch 3 turn. Work one more row of dc, end off. Rep on opposite side of belt. Wrap each flap around its bar, taking into consideration how the closure works best and your right- or left-handedness. Sew in place with yarn and tapestry needle.

RIPPLE RESORT MINI

In the very first design in this book I discussed my desire to work with gathered fabric in crochet, and this design takes the concept farther. How easy it would be, thought I, if a dress could be made that's just a rectangle which gathers near the neckline. In truth, I saw a dress like that in a fancy Soho shop, but as it was made of a very thin, gauzy fabric I had no idea if it could work in crochet. Throwing a crocheted poncho around my neck, the result was still off the mark but, with a lighter, more airy fabric, it seemed promising enough to give it a stab. With this DK yarn and a pretty, open work ripple pattern, I think it worked!

The steep curve of this ripple pattern would make complex shaping daunting, and luckily this design requires none. While in the past I have made many tailored crochet garments, I now appreciate how well simpler garments fit if the magic ingredient of drape is in the mix. The fabric finds the curves in our body and hangs in flattering lines around them.

RIPPLE
RESORT MINI

skill level: easy

size

Small/Medium (Large, X-Large)

finished measurements

Chest/Hip, 37½ (45, 52½)"

materials

RY Classic Luxury Cotton DK, (1.75 ounces/104
  yards, 50 grams/95 meters per ball):
  #256 Broncho — 10 (12, 14) balls
Size F-5 (3.75 mm) crochet hook
2–3 yds ½"-wide ribbon or cord

gauge

1 patt rep = 3¾"
6 rows = 2½"

stitching tip

If you like to work with even finer weight yarns
and lacy stitches, you can adapt this pattern and
make a lovely variation. Simply create a rectangle
that's wide enough to fit around your bust or hips
(whichever is wider) — remember if it's in two
pieces as in this design, divide that measurement
in half, or you can work it all in one piece and put
a seam at the back. Work even to your desired
length, gather it up at the neck with a pretty ribbon or cord, and take it for a night out!

wavy pattern stitch

Multiple of 19 + 1

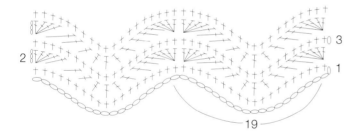

Row 1: Sc in 2nd ch from hook and in each ch across.
Row 2: Ch 3, 4 dc in first sc, *(dc in next sc, sk 1 sc) 8 times, dc in next sc, (5 dc in next sc) 2 times, rep from * across, ending (5 dc in next sc) once only, ch 1, turn.
Row 3: Sc in each dc across, sc in tch, ch 3, turn.
Rep rows 2 and 3 for patt.

instructions

Dress (Make 2)

Ch 96 (115, 134).
Work in Wavy Pattern for 28¼" or desired length ending on row 3 — 5 (6, 7) patt reps.
Note: Measure from collar bone to determine desired length.

finishing

Sew side seams from RS with mattress stitch, stopping 7 (8, 9)" from top edge. Sew corners of front and back pieces together at shoulders by looping yarn around end stitches several times and securing in tails well. Beginning at center front of dress, weave ribbon or cord around 2nd to last row of work, over and under 2 dc at a time, ending again at center front. The ends of the cord or ribbon will tie in front.

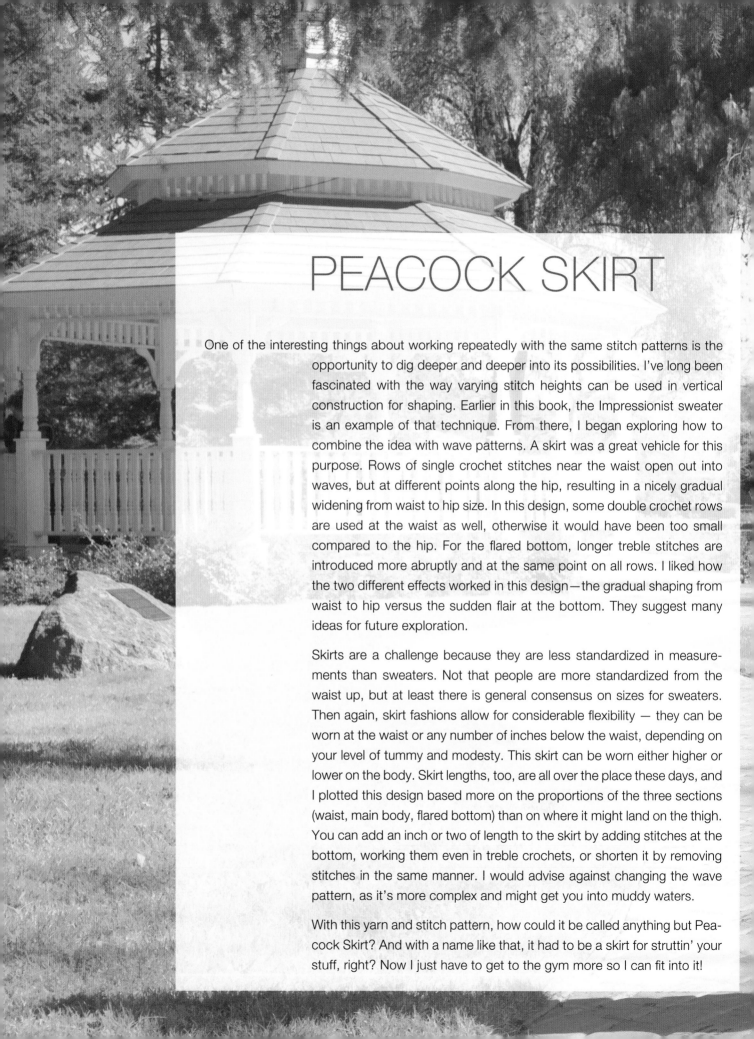

PEACOCK SKIRT

One of the interesting things about working repeatedly with the same stitch patterns is the opportunity to dig deeper and deeper into its possibilities. I've long been fascinated with the way varying stitch heights can be used in vertical construction for shaping. Earlier in this book, the Impressionist sweater is an example of that technique. From there, I began exploring how to combine the idea with wave patterns. A skirt was a great vehicle for this purpose. Rows of single crochet stitches near the waist open out into waves, but at different points along the hip, resulting in a nicely gradual widening from waist to hip size. In this design, some double crochet rows are used at the waist as well, otherwise it would have been too small compared to the hip. For the flared bottom, longer treble stitches are introduced more abruptly and at the same point on all rows. I liked how the two different effects worked in this design—the gradual shaping from waist to hip versus the sudden flair at the bottom. They suggest many ideas for future exploration.

Skirts are a challenge because they are less standardized in measurements than sweaters. Not that people are more standardized from the waist up, but at least there is general consensus on sizes for sweaters. Then again, skirt fashions allow for considerable flexibility — they can be worn at the waist or any number of inches below the waist, depending on your level of tummy and modesty. This skirt can be worn either higher or lower on the body. Skirt lengths, too, are all over the place these days, and I plotted this design based more on the proportions of the three sections (waist, main body, flared bottom) than on where it might land on the thigh. You can add an inch or two of length to the skirt by adding stitches at the bottom, working them even in treble crochets, or shorten it by removing stitches in the same manner. I would advise against changing the wave pattern, as it's more complex and might get you into muddy waters.

With this yarn and stitch pattern, how could it be called anything but Peacock Skirt? And with a name like that, it had to be a skirt for struttin' your stuff, right? Now I just have to get to the gym more so I can fit into it!

PEACOCK SKIRT

skill level: easy

size
Small (Medium, Large, X-Large)

finished measurements
Waist, 28 (32, 36, 40)"
Hip, 35 (40, 45, 50)"
Length, 20"

materials

Trendsetter Tonalita Yarn, 52% wool, 48% acrylic,
(1.75 ounces/100 yards, 50 grams/91 meters per ball):
  #2396 Starry Night — 7 balls
Size H-8 (5.00 mm) crochet hook or size needed to
  obtain gauge
Size F-5 (3.75 mm) crochet hook for trim
Three ⅝" black snaps
Black button thread

gauge
14 sts (2 sc, 2 hdc, 2 dc, 3 tr, 2 dc, 2 hdc, sc), and 6
rows in patt = 2¼"

pattern stitch

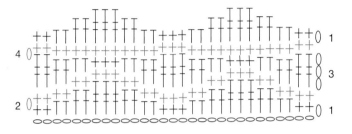

Wave 1

All sizes: With larger hook, ch 67.

Row 1: Sc in 2nd ch from hook, 9 sc *2 sc, 2 hdc, 2 dc, 3 tr, 2 dc, sc; rep from * twice, sc, ending with 13 tr, turn — 66 sts.

Row 2: Ch 1, sc in each st across, turn.

Row 3: Ch 1, 17 sc, *2 sc, 2 hdc, 2 dc, 3 tr, 2 dc, 2 hdc, sc; rep from * once, 2 sc, 2 hdc, 2 dc, ending with 15 tr, turn.

Row 4: Ch 4 (counts as first tr), 14 tr, 2 dc, 2 hdc, sc, *2 sc, 2 hdc, 2 dc, 3 tr; 2 dc, 2 hdc, sc; rep from * once, 18 sc, turn.

Row 5: Ch 1, sc in each st across, ending sc in tch, turn.

Row 6: Ch 4 (counts as first tr), 12 tr, *2 sc, 2 hdc, 2 dc, 3 tr, 2 dc, 2 hdc, sc; rep from * once, 2 sc, 2 hdc, 2 dc, 3 tr, 16 sc, turn.

Wave 2

Row 7: Ch 3 (counts as first dc), 15 dc, 3 tr, 2 dc, 2 hdc, sc, *2 sc, 2 hdc, 2 dc, 3 tr, 2 dc, 2 hdc, sc; rep from * once, sc, 13 tr, turn — 66 sts.

Rows 8–12: Rep rows 2–6 of wave 1.

Wave 3

Rows 1–5: Rep rows 1–5 of Wave 1, working into st of previous row, rather than foundation chain. This row will mirror the previous row completed.

Row 6: Ch 4 (counts as first tr) 12 tr, *2 sc, 2 hdc, 2 dc, 3 tr, 2 dc, 2 hdc, sc, rep from * twice, ending with 11 sc.

Skirt

(Worked in one continuous piece)

With larger hook, ch 67, turn.

Rows 1–6: Work Wave 1.

Rows 7–12: Work Wave 2.

Rows 13 (13, 13, 13)–36 (42, 48, 54): Rep Wave 2 — four (5, 6, 7) more times.

Rows 37 (43, 49, 55)–42 (48, 54, 60): Work Wave 3.

At this point, half of the skirt is completed. Do not end off, but continue by repeating rows 1–42 (55, 60) again. Row 1 will be worked into st of prev row. Do not end off, but continue to closure flap.

Closure Flap

Turn, sc in each of the next 18 sts.
Rep this row 3 additional times, end off.
Weave in all ends at waist of skirt.

finishing

Using smaller hook, with RS facing, work evenly spaced sc trim along the top edge of the skirt. You can work tightly to decrease the waist measurement, if necessary.

The seam goes at the back of the skirt and can be sewn with mattress stitch from either side. Sew seam up to the closure flap. Sew 3 snaps vertically along inside edge of closure flap, male side to flap, female side to corresponding points of skirt. Sew snaps very close to edge using black button thread.

CARIBE COVERUP

In keeping with the aim of presenting a variety of yarn fibers in this book, I was eager to include one of the new bamboo yarns. A few swatches convinced me that bamboo has a special springiness that's most suitable to casual wear. It's lighter than cotton and unlike some fragile or temperamental fibers, it's resilient. In search of unique ripple patterns, I came upon one I liked in "365 Crochet Stitches a Year" a perpetual calendar compiled by my crochet mentors, Jean Leinhauser and Rita Weiss. Since the pattern is quite intricate, it is alternated with a much simpler stitch. This provides relief to the eye, as well as to the crocheter making this piece, and helps the ripples stand out more.

Working on this pattern brought home a point I ponder from time to time: the fact that crochet draws on many different parts of the brain — engineering, mathematics, the ability to visualize balance and harmony in color and composition. Designing has made me more aware of those parts of my own brain which are more facile than others. For example, having been a musician since I was a child, I find it much easier to memorize musical patterns (even fairly difficult ones) than it is to memorize complex stitch patterns. Yet for some of my crochet colleagues, it's a piece of cake! Nevertheless, I really enjoy a pattern like this because I get to admire the marvelous architecture of this stitch, which I will attempt to describe.

Row 1 sets up the single crochet border that edges the ripple, and it will be repeated at the outside edge. This border has the effect of setting off the ripple pattern, which takes shape over four rows. The ripple proper begins in row 2, with 8 trebles and chains forming a fan for the upward curve, alternating with single crochet where the pattern dips. In the next row the fan pattern is amplified: in row 1 the fan contains 8 stitches; in this row it has 12. The dip between fans is now dc, sc, dc, with no chains between them, creating a more pronounced ripple. The final ripple row is "upside down," with shorter stitches topping off the hills gradually moving to taller stitches for the dips. The center of the dip is accented by an upside-down "V" formed by a tr2tog. This row is worked in the front loops, making the ripple much more visible. What ingenuity it took for someone to come up with this marvelous pattern! Another feature of this design is the multidirectional rows: horizontal from the bottom to just under the breast, vertical from there to the shoulder. Basically, it's two rectangles sewn together, proving, I hope you'll agree, that simple can be pretty cute!

I like to think this piece is worthy of the fanciest beach, be it a Caribbean paradise or the French Riviera, but I plan to wear it at Coney Island Beach, right here in New York, as soon as the weather warms up.

CARIBE COVERUP

skill level: intermediate

size
Small/Medium (Large, X-Large)

finished measurements
Bust, 36 (45, 54)"

materials

RYC Yarns Bamboo Soft, (1.75 ounces/112 yards, 50 grams/102 meters per ball):
#100 Cream — 11 (12, 13) balls
Size E-4 (3.50 mm) crochet hook or size needed to obtain gauge

gauge
1 patt rep (6 rows) = 2¼" x 1¾"

ripple lace stitch

Multiple of 12 + 2

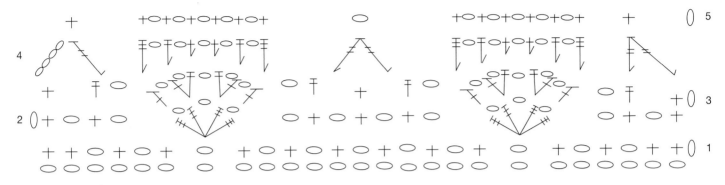

Row 1: Sc in 2nd ch from hook, sc in next ch, *ch 1, sk next ch, sc in next ch, rep from * across, ending with sc in last ch, turn.

Row 2: Ch 1, sc in 1st sc, ch 1, sk next sc, sc in next ch-1 sp, ch 1, sk next (sc, ch-1 sp, sc), work (tr, ch 1) 4 times in next ch-1 sp, * sk next (sc, ch-1 sp, sc), (sc in next ch-1 sp, ch 1) 3 times, work (tr, ch 1) 4 times in next ch-1 sp, rep from * ending sk next (sc, ch-1 sp, sc), sc in next ch-1 sp, sk next sc, ch 1, sc in last sc, turn.

Row 3: Ch 1, sc in first sc, *dc in next sc, ch 1, dc in next tr, ch 1, (dc, ch 1) 2 times in each of next 2 tr, dc in next tr, ch 1, dc in next sc, sc in next sc, rep from * across, turn.

Row 4: Ch 4, sk 1st sc, FLtr in next 2dc, ch 1, FLdc in next dc, ch 1 (FLsc in next dc, ch 1) twice, FLdc in next dc, ch 1, FLtr in next dc, sk next ch 1 sp, *FLtr2tog over next 3 st, FLtr in next dc, ch 1, FLdc in next dc, ch 1, (FLsc in next dc, ch 1) twice, FLdc in next dc, ch 1, FLtr in next dc, rep from * to last 2 sts, FL tr2tog, turn.

Row 5: Ch 1, sc in first st and in next tr, (ch 1, sk next ch-1 sp, sc in next st) 5 times, * ch 1, sk next st, sc in next st, (ch 1, sk next ch-1 sp, sc in next st) 5 times, rep from * ending sc in tch, turn.

Rep rows 1–5 for pattern.

special stitch

Front loop treble 2 stitches together (FLtr2tog): worked over next 3 st as follows: *Wrap yarn around hook 3 times, insert hook in front lp of next dc and draw up a lp, (yo and draw through 2 lps) 2 times* (2 lps on hook), sk next sc, rep from * to * once (3 lps on hook), yo, draw through all 3 lps on hook.

instructions

Body (Make 2)

Ch 98 (122,146).

Rows 1–5: Work in Ripple Lace Pattern, turn — 8 (10, 12) patt reps.

Row 6–10: Ch 3, dc in 2nd sc, *ch 1, sk ch-1 sp, dc in next sc, rep from * across ending dc in last sc, turn.

Rows 11–30: Ch 1, rep rows 1–10, 2 times.

Rows 31–35: Ch 1, rep rows 1–5, end off.

Sleeve and Yoke
Right Panel
Ch 122, 122, 146

Rows 1–10: Follow directions for body for 10 rows; there will be 10(10, 12) patt reps; in dc rows there will be 62 (62, 74) dc.

Medium Only
Rows 11–15: Rep row 6.

Large Only
Rows 11–20: Rep rows 1–10.

All Sizes
Rows 11–15 (16–20, 21–25): Work ripple patt across.

Front Yoke
Next row: Rep row 6 of body but completing only 24 (24, 30) dc, ch 3, turn.
Cont in (dc, ch 1) patt for 6 (6, 9) more rows, end off.

Back Yoke
Tie on at unworked end of row where front yoke begins, work 28 (28, 34) dc in patt across, ch 3, turn.
Cont in (dc, ch 1) patt for 6 (6, 9) more rows, end off.

Left Panel
Follow directions for Right panel up to Front yoke.

Back Yoke
Next row: Rep row 6 of body completing 28 (28, 34) dc, ch 3, turn.
Cont in (dc, ch 1) patt for 6 (6, 9) more rows, end off.

Front Yoke
Tie on at unworked end of row where back yoke begins, work 24 (24, 30) dc in patt across, ch 3, turn.
Cont in (dc, ch 1) patt for more 6 (6, 9) more rows, end off.

finishing

Sew the yoke pieces together at Center Back. Carefully pin the yoke to the body, making certain the center meets the exact center of the body. There will be some extra fabric in the body to be eased in. Sew the front and back yokes to the body from WS. Sew corners of front neckline pieces together.

Cord

With a smaller hook of your choice, make a chain about 40–60" in length. Do not weave in the ends. This chain will be woven through the top of the body. Find the exact center of the front and begin weaving here. Place a tapestry needle on one end in order to weave the chain in and out of the second to last row of work on the body (the one that has tr stitches). It is done on this row, with its tall stitches, making it far easier than weaving it through the last row of single crochet stitches. After weaving in the cord, weave in the ends.

The sleeves are left open at the sides for beachwear, but if you'd like a more tailored look, you can sew seams up the sides to the desired length of armhole.

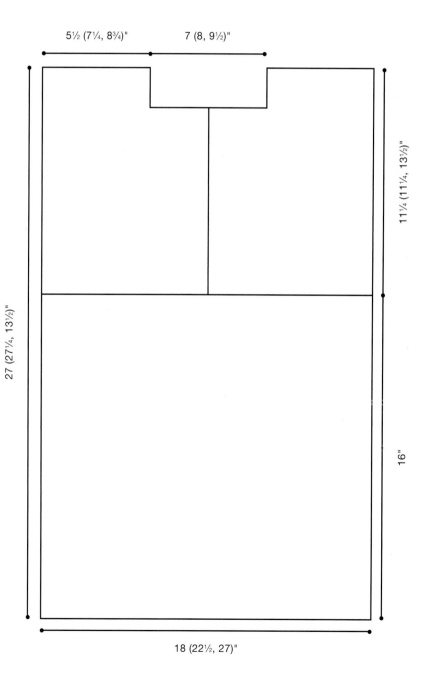

FRUITCASE

After many months of working with diamonds, waves, and ripple stitches, combining them in one project seemed inevitable. The trick was how to get them to match up one next to the other. My first stitch choice for this projects was the wavy ripple, one of my favorite stitches. Since a computer case can't have a wave at its edge, I was working on getting a flat edge by using graduated longer and shorter stitches in the row next to the ripple, and *voila!* Here was a wave! Unintended solutions are always the best, aren't they?

The other idea I had for this design was creating a patchwork effect, but without lots of sewing. I decided to use color blocks, each with a wave in a different color at its center. I divided the case into two main sections, worked in different directions—the bottom in vertical rows, the top horizontal. For the latter, I used another popular ripple stitch that resembles a wedge. That stitch and the diamond stitch pattern adapted to each other quite well. I must lay some of the inspiration for this fruity case to the riotous and vast selection of colors available in Tahki Stacy Charles Classic Cotton.

I found working with these shapes combined with color work was very exciting, as the interplay of geometry and color is suggestive of ethnic and folk art that I love. It's another avenue I intend to take a long stroll down in future crochet journeys!

FRUITCASE

skill level: intermediate

finished measurements

12" x 10" x 1½"

materials

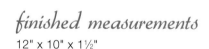

Tahki Stacy Charles Cotton Classic Yarn (1.75 ounces/108
  yards, 50 grams/100 meters per ball)1 ball each of:
  #3432 Burgundy (A)
  #3724 Leaf Green (B)
  #3549 Mustard (C)
  #3358 Tobacco Brown (D)
  #3407 Dark Brick (E)
  #3540 Mango (F)
Size D-3 (3.25 mm) crochet hook or size needed to
  obtain gauge
3 yds (¾"–1") matching fabric strap
Buckle to fit strap
Large shank button

gauge

Rows 1–3 = 6" x 1¾"
Note: Each section of 8 rows should be 4" x 6". For a
smaller case (11" x 9" x 1"), tighten your gauge as follows:
rows 1–3 = 1¾" x 5½". The upper portion of the case will be
correspondingly smaller when working with a tighter gauge.
For the side panel, use tr rather than dtr and a ¾" width strap.

special stitches

Tall double crochet (tall dc): Same as regular dc, but pull up the first loop height to about ⅜". This will ensure that fabric doesn't get pinched.

Double treble stitch (dtr): Wrap yarn around hook 3 times, insert hook in designated stitch, yo and draw up loop, (yo and draw through 2 loops on hook) 4 times.

Side 1 (Front of Case)

With A, ch 31.

Row 1: *Tr in 5th ch from hook, 2 dc, 2 hdc, 2 sc, 2 hdc, 2 dc, 3 tr, 2 dc**, 2 hdc, sc, 2 dc, rep from * ending last rep at **, 2 tr, turn — 28 sts.

Row 2: Ch 3, 2 dc in first st, *3 dc, dc3tog, dc3tog, 3 dc**, (3 dc in next st) 2 times, rep from * ending last rep at **, 3 dc in tch.

Row 3: Ch 1, rep row 2, change to color B, carrying unused yarn along side, turn.

Row 4: Ch 1, *2 sc, 2 hdc, 2 dc, 2 tr, 2 dc, 2 hdc, 2 sc, rep from * across, turn.

Row 5: Rep row 4, pick up color A, turn.

Row 6: Ch 3, *dc3tog, 3 dc, (3 dc in next st) 2 times, 3 dc, dc-3tog, rep from * across, turn.

Row 7: Rep row 6, turn.

Row 8: Ch 4, rep row 1, working into st of prev row rather than foundation ch.

Rows 9–24: Rep rows 1–8 twice with this color sequence: CDC, EFE.

Turn work 90 degress and tie on with color D at right edge, ch 1. You will be working into sides of rows.

Row 1: Sc in first row, *9 tall dc in next row, sk next row, sc in next row, (at the point of "leaf"), sk next 2 rows, 9 tall dc in next row, sk next row, (one panel completed) sc in next row, rep from * across, ending sc in base of foundation ch at left edge, change to color B, turn — 6 patt reps.

Row 2: Ch 1, sc2tog over (sc, dc) 3 sc, 3 sc in next dc, 4 sc, sk sc**, 4 sc, rep from * ending last rep at **, 3 sc, sc2tog, turn — 66 sts.

Row 3: Ch 1, sc2tog, 3 sc, 3 sc in next sc, 4 sc, sk 2 sc**, 4 sc, rep from * ending last rep at**, 3 sc, sc2tog, change to color C, turn.

Rows 4–5: Rep rows 2 and 3, change to color A.

Row 6: Ch 3, dc4tog over next 4 sc, ch 3 loosely, sc in next sc, ch 3 loosely, dc10tog over next 10 sc, ch 3, sc in next sc, ch 3, ending dc5tog over last 5 sc, turn.

Row 7: Ch 3, 4 dc in eye, sc in next sc, *9 dc in next eye, sc in next sc, rep from * across ending 5 dc in last eye, change to color F, turn.

Row 8: Ch 1, 2 sc in first dc, 4 sc, sk next sc, *4 sc, 3 sc in next dc, 4 sc, sk sc, rep from * across, ending 4 sc, 2 sc in tch, turn.

Row 9: Ch 1, 2 sc in first sc, 4 sc, sk next 2 sc, *4 sc, 3 sc in next sc, 4 sc, sk sc, rep from * across, ending 4 sc, 2 sc in last sc, change to color D, turn.

Rows 10–11: Rep row 9 (don't worry if edges seem to be widening, they will be pulled in by next row), change to color E, turn.

Row 12: Ch 1, sc in first sc, *ch 3, dc10tog over next 10 sc, sc in next dc, rep from * across.

Row 13: Ch 3, *sc, 3 sc in ch-3 sp, sc in eye, 3 sc in ch-3 sp, rep from * across, end off.

Side 2 (Back of Case)

Rep rows 1–24 instructions for side 1 using this color sequence:

Rows 1–3: Color F.
Rows 4–5: Color A.
Rows 6–8: Color F.
Rows 9–11: Color B.
Rows 12–13: Color E.
Rows 14–16: Color B.
Rows 17–19: Color D.
Rows 20–21: Color C.
Rows 22–24: Color D.

After turning work, work rows 1–12 using this color sequence:

Row 1: Color A.
Rows 2–3: Color C.
Rows 4–5: Color E.
Rows 6–7: Color B.
Rows 8–9: Color A.
Rows 10–11: Color F.
Row 12: Color D.

Do not change color, continue with top of side 2 and front flap as follows:

Row 13: Ch 1, sc in sc, *9 dc in next eye, sc in sc, rep from * to end.

Rows 14–19: Rep rows 2–7 using this color sequence: C, E, B.

Rows 20–24: Rep rows 8–12 using this color sequence: A, F, D, end off.

Side and Bottom Panel

Weave in all ends. Steam block both pieces to flatten and gently pull edges to even them out. Take care not to stretch fabric too much, or it will not fit your computer! Cotton stretches easily, so a gentle pulling and patting while steaming will yield the best results.

Row 1: With Side 1 RS facing, tie on D at top left, ch 1; work evenly spaced sc all around side, bottom and other side. DO NOT work extra sc in corners, as the fabric should curl rather than lie flat. Keep stitch counts on either side consistent. End off.

Row 2: To keep fronts of stitches facing, tie on again at beg of row 1 with B, ch 5. Depending on how your computer measures at the sides, work dtr or tr in each sc all around, again with no extra stitches at corners. Change color to D, ch 1, turn.

Row 3: This row is a sc seam to connect the 2 sides of the work together. Place RS of both pieces facing each other; you will work with WS facing. Beginning at top of Side 1 and row 12 of Side 2, work sc seam, picking up 2 strands of each side, joining Side 2 to side panel just made. Take care to match patterns on two sides of bag. When you reach the end of side 1, secure loop on safety pin. Turn work right side out and examine your seam. If it looks fine, continue with same yarn and work sc border around front flap of bag. Work up along the side; work 1 extra st at corner, if necessary to prevent curling edge. At the top edge, work into row 24 as follows:

Row 25: *Sc in sc, 3 sc in ch-3 sp, sc in eye, 3 sc in ch-3 sp, rep twice, sc in next sc, ch 10 for button loop. (**Note:** You may need more or fewer chains, depending on the size of your button). Test this and make a loop that is just long enough to get around the button, rep from * (there are 2 sc in the center, the point from which the button loop extends to the end) turn corner and work sc edging down opposite side of flap, end off.

We are almost there folks! Another round of weaving in ends comes next. Now take the strap and weave it in and out of the row of dtr or tr in the side panels of the case, beginning by inserting the strap under the 3rd and 4th sts, over next 5 sts, under next 2 sts, etc. to end. Feel free to experiment and see what you like best as to how many stitches you want above and below the strap.

stitching tips
More About Edging

When working the body of a piece of crochet, keeping even tension is usually our goal. We want those stitches looking even all the way through and strive to maintain our gauge so that the measurements turn out as planned. When it comes to edging, however, I believe good crochet technique requires some flexibility in tension. Stitches may need to get tighter or looser to fit the correct number of stitches into a given area. You also need to judge what looks best and learn to trust your eye. It can be a real challenge to follow the seemingly simple instruction: "Work evenly spaced sc edging around work." Working into the sides of rows, stitches of varying lengths, chain spaces, and corners all require an observant eye and the willingness to rip and repeat. For example, in this piece the final rows of sc are worked into ch-3 spaces, to me, this edging looked best when the single crochet stitches were worked rather tightly, so that they wouldn't cram the ch-3 spaces and bulge. I also found that working around the corners of the flap did not require any extra corner stitches, because the stitches appeared to fill out the corner without them. This was simply a matter of noticing exactly what happened as I was working it. If I don't like what I see, I rip and try something else. In other words, a little "rule-breaking" is OK; stitching is not like graph paper, and what ends up looking best is best.

Good edging is also more of a challenge with color work, as in this piece, because you can see clearly where the edging emerges from the work. If you aren't consistent in how many strands you pick up, the inside edge of the border looks strange. It's easy when working into the tops of stitches, but problematic when working into the sides of long stitches — double crochets and taller. I generally like to pick up two strands from the sides of stitches. For turning chains, I also pick up only 2 strands, rather than work around the whole chain. If you work around the entire stitch, you'll get an unwanted hole, while picking up only one strand can end up stretching the yarn and yielding a floppy edging. Yes, crocheters, these little points of polish are well worth your time and effort for a truly fabulous finished product. Think of these tips as "crochet finishing school."

author's note
DORA OHRENSTEIN

I taught myself to crochet during the 1970s, when I was a hippie living on a houseboat in Amsterdam. I made some pretty things without really knowing what I was doing. To my suprise and delight, some items were sold in a boutique. Then I put down the hook for 25 years while I pursued a career as a singer. I toured the world as vocalist of the Philip Glass Ensemble for ten years, and had many other great singing "gigs." That life has given me excitement, travel, and much more to be thankful for, and I continue to perform and teach singing. I started to crochet again in 2004 and attended a CGOA conference that summer in Manchester, New Hampshire. There I met two of the *grande dames* of needlework, Jean Leinhauser and Rita Weiss, who encouraged me to sell my designs and actually bought several items "off my back." Since then, I've had designs printed in several books and magazines. I've also published historical and technical articles on crochet in various magazines and in my own webzine, Crochet Insider, on the web at www.crochetinsider.com.

Crochet Insider was launched in 2006 as a quarterly e-zine dedicated to presenting high quality crochet in all its amazing incarnations: couture fashion, art and sculpture, historic and traditional styles, and cutting edge experimental work. As founder and editor, I have had a great time interviewing some of the needlework industry's leading figures for its pages.

I get great pleasure and stimulation from the creativity and challenge of creating with crochet. There's so much to learn about the business and the craft and never enough time! Becoming part of the community of "people of the yarn" (a charming expression I stole from Vogue Knitting Editor Adina Klein) has given me wonderful new friends and colleagues.

I live in Manhattan Upper West Side, across the street from the Museum of Natural History and one block from Central Park, with my piano, hooks, books, and more yarn than a studio apartment ought to have in it.

Published by:
the art of everyday living

Copyright ©2008 by Leisure Arts, Inc.,
5701 Ranch Drive, Little Rock,
AR 72223
www.leisurearts.com
www.crochetinsider.com

Production Team:
• Art Director: **Basha Kooler**
• Senior Graphic Designer: **Ashley Rocha**
• Photographer: **Dianne Woods**